PEACE BEHIND THE WIRE

THE WIRE

A NONVIOLENT RESOLUTION

THE POWER OF PEACE PROJECT

KIT CUMMINGS

LOGIX®

Alpharetta, GA

ISBN: 978-1-61005-616-8
Library of Congress Control Number: 2015911141

10 9 8 7 6 5 4 3 2   0 1 0 5 1 8

Printed in the United States of America

♾This paper meets the requirements of ANSI/NISO Z39.48-1992 (Permanence of Paper)

This book is dedicated to my father Johnny Howard Cummings.
I miss you dad, but I know that you are always with me.
Rest in peace, I love you.

"Darkness cannot drive out darkness; only light can do that. Hate cannot drive out hate; only love can do that."

–Martin Luther King, Jr.

CONTENTS

FOREWORD

For I was hungry and you gave me food; I was thirsty, and you gave me drink; I was a stranger and you welcomed me; I was naked and you clothed me; I was sick and you visited me; I was in prison and you came to me.

Blessed are the peacemakers, for they shall be called sons of God.
                                                    –Jesus of Nazareth

I remember when Kit Cummings first told me about his work with youth around the country and his vision for the Power of Peace Project. He spoke of the influence that Gandhi, King, Mandela, and Mother Teresa had on his thinking. He talked about how God was at the center of everything he was doing. My faith was personally challenged after I read the passages above. I immediately realized that I had to get behind Kit and his mission. What he and others were doing to help bring peace to those in prison and to those who had violence in their hearts was truly inspiring.

In his book, *Peace Behind the Wire*, Kit gives us a look into the journey he has been on to be a peacemaker in the lives of young people who are at great risk. I've watched Kit's work with many leaders, schools, correctional systems, law enforcement agencies, and community organizations across the country and around the world. This has become a youth peace movement with many victories and success stories along the way. I have seen the impact of Kit's passion for the struggle, and I am reminded that change happens when one person decides that enough is enough. The commitment to peace that we are witnessing by those who once had hatred and anger in their hearts is amazing.

Dr. King spoke about peace when he received the Noble Peace Prize. He said, "Sooner or later all the people of the world will have to discover a way to live in peace." This statement by Dr. King is at the center of *Peace Behind the Wire*. King goes on to say, "Peace is more precious than diamonds, silver, and gold." This expression is what the Power of Peace Project is all about. I have enjoyed watching POPP develop and grow, and I am astonished by the results. The challenge is for all who read this book to join Kit and unleash the Power of Peace.

To my brother, friend, and peacemaker—may God continue to bless you and your important work. Thank you for your journey toward finding Peace Behind the Wire!

Antonio B. Boyd
President & CEO
The Think Tank Consulting Group

In 2005, South Carolina Governor Mark Sanford appointed Antonio to the South Carolina Commission for national and community service. In 2006, the White House selected Antonio to represent South Carolina as one of the state's fifteen delegates to the commission on aging. Senator Lyndsay Graham chose Antonio for two consecutive years as delegate to the US Senate's African American Leadership Summit. During the Clinton administration, Antonio worked with Sylvia Panetta, wife of former Chief of Staff Leon Panetta, and Vice President Al Gore on the president's Crime Prevention Council. Antonio serves on the board of the South Carolina Association of Non-Profit Organizations and as a past president of the Columbia Luncheon Club, one of South Carolina's oldest civil rights and community relations organizations. At the community level, Antonio started the Buffalo Soldier Youth Development Corporation to help disadvantaged youth express themselves through music instead of violence.

ACKNOWLEDGMENTS

I would like to thank the very first wardens, chaplains, and principals who partnered with the Power of Peace Project and helped make this dream a reality. Clay Tatum, Jason Bunting, Mary Berghuis, Onesiphorus Burrel, and Jacquelyn Whitt, your dedication, sacrifice, and service to the men and women you lead and protect has inspired me. You believed in POPP before anyone even knew about it, and I am eternally grateful. May God bless and watch over you and everyone under your care. Peace be with you.

INTRODUCTION

On January 18, 2011, twelve men inside Georgia's most violent and dangerous maximum security prison signed a peace pledge. They signed in honor of Dr. Martin Luther King's birthday and in celebration of the twenty-fifth anniversary of MLK Day. They signed because they were challenged, and even dared, to see if it was possible to live peacefully for forty days in a prison that had over half of the general population active and affiliated in dangerous gangs. They signed because they desired a better quality of life and they wanted to do easier time. These twelve original members were white, black, and Latino; Christian and Muslim; old and young. But they had one very important thing in common: they all desperately desired peace. Quickly the word began to spread and soon gang leaders were getting involved in what was being called "Peace at Hays." Fights were broken up, hits were called off, and major escalating situations were put down. Peace came to that institution for a miraculous season and this violent prison won Institution of the Year in the State of Georgia in 2011. However, the peace wouldn't last as a gang war tore through several state prisons the following year and four killings in six weeks locked that prison down. But an idea had been born and taken root, and hope and light had come to a dark and desperate place. If given the chance, would convicts in other prisons and other states choose peace over violence? If given the inspiration and motivation, could hated, feared, and forgotten men truly change? This book tells the story of how those twelve men started a peace movement that is now spreading to prisons and schools across the country. Dr. King's dream of "restoring our beloved community" is happening in the most unexpected places. This is an idea whose time has come: a nonviolent resolution.

This was an idea, which led to an experiment that became a program that evolved into a movement. This is a true story and the young history of an organization that is called the Power of Peace Project (POPP). This series of forty day projects is bringing peace and resolution to dysfunctional institutions, whether it be prisons, schools, churches, or wounded communities. POPP intends to institutionalize nonviolence. I will begin each of the next twenty-two chapters with a story that highlights a significant point in the journey or a turning point for the movement. Then I will go on to chronicle the Power of Peace history and also explain the simple but powerful steps that make up the POPP process. This is going to be a roller coaster ride: vivid accounts of transformation and redemption, heartache and pain, danger and fear, breakthroughs and freedom. You will see that this project is working and the news is spreading quickly. We'll be coming to your town soon, because everybody wants peace, and our world is hungry for it like never before.

Original Members from Inside the First Three POPP Prisons

The Mighty Men of Muskegon

The Hays Inmate Council

The Marion Movement

CHAPTER 1
PSYCHO UNDER THE STAIRS

I am standing under a dark stairway, and out of sight from anyone else in our group. A man stands uncomfortably close, so close that I can smell his breath. His head is shaved, and there are tattoos on his face. His eyes shift back and forth and his body moves uncomfortably. He has been in this place for a long time and he will not leave during his natural life. He goes by the name of "Psycho" and he lives in an eight-by-ten-foot cell in a place that those in the free world rarely see. He has asked if he can talk to me, because he has an important question to ask. This is the first time we have officially met, and we are on his turf. This is Alabama's death row. Twenty-two men currently live there and they have all received the law's most severe consequence: they will live out the rest of their lives there, and they will all die one day by lethal injection. He tells me that he is indeed guilty of the crimes that he has been convicted of and that he deserves what he has coming to him—an admission which is somewhat rare in this place. I have spent several hours this afternoon with this misfit band of brothers, and on this day they will memorialize a close friend that they have all lost just the week before. This is my first trip to "the row," though I have made a number of trips since that unforgettable Saturday afternoon. His eyes begin to moisten and tears fall over his teardrop tattoos. His voice quivers as he begins to ask the question. I turn to the right to see if anyone else can still see us, which they cannot. My eyes turn back to him and into his deep stare.

"I have a question for you, preacher," Psycho says in a hushed tone.

1

"What can I do for you?" I reply.

"I want to get right with Him before they take me, and this is what I need to know: can your God save a man like me?" Tears fill his eyes.

That question digs deep into my heart. Here was a man that the world hates, fears, and that many have forgotten, though some never will, waiting on a phone call that he hopes will never come. He is asking me the age old question that so many have asked before. How do I get past what I have done, the choices that I have made, and the way that I have lived my life? My life's work has become all about how to help people answer that question, and find a way to change. To make amends, heal broken relationships, find meaning and purpose in their lives—and make things right, for themselves and to this wounded world. This random but powerful interaction caused a shift inside of me and got me thinking about solutions.

The Philly Epiphany

The idea came as I was standing at the back of an auditorium in Philadelphia on December 5, 2010. I had just delivered a keynote speech for a large international non-profit organization. My mind was clear, and I felt alive, the way that speakers feel when they have just knocked it out of the park—sweaty, high and in the moment. Martin Luther King's picture flashed up onto the screen and the participants at this conference were being challenged to go back to our cities and do something in honor of MLK Day the following month. Then my life-altering thought arrived: *What if we signed a peace pledge inside Georgia's most violent prison in honor of Dr. King's upcoming birthday?* It was clear and simple, and I'm so glad that I did not overthink it. It made so much sense to me. Maybe these violent inmates would not stand down for their warden, the officers, their families, for me, or anybody else; but just maybe they would do it for Dr. King (he still commands great respect from men of all colors and ages). On January 18 the following month, our country would celebrate the twenty-fifth anniversary of MLK Day becoming a national holiday. This was perfect timing—it gave me about a month to try and get approval from the warden and find my first participants. But could I find inmates who were willing to try it, and would the warden buy into the experiment? As I flew back to Atlanta, ideas flew through my mind. I created seven steps that would form the pledge and I began to imagine what might motivate men to change, men who live inside one of the most violent prisons in the nation: twelve hundred men living in tight quarters with enemies, mental health cases, violent offenders, life sentence convicts, and many with nothing to lose. The experiment was based on my belief that human beings are created to live in peace, and if given the choice, would choose peace over violence. I believe that we are all created to live in community, to be fathers and mothers, and to take care of the weak and elderly. I believe in universal laws and principles that were set in place by a loving and benevolent, all powerful Creator, who created us in His image. Based on these convictions, I decided that I would give it a try. But first I had to convince the warden.

Hays State Prison sits in the middle of nowhere in the beautiful foothills of the North Georgia mountains, near the Tennessee and Alabama state lines. If you drive down a little road across from the Walmart, you find a self-contained world that many don't even know exists. Twelve hundred men live in a place that none of the sixty-thousand inmates locked up in the State of Georgia ever wants to end up. Hays has a reputation as a place where men do some of the hardest time imaginable. Four out of five inmates are doing fifteen years or more; a third are doing life; a third are classified mental health cases; and as many as half are suspected of being actively affiliated with gangs and criminal organizations. When men get off the bus after the long ride from Jackson, they are afraid of Hays, whether they admit it or not. Several years ago there was an escape and two men got over the razor wire. After several very anxious days in that small community, they were rounded up and sent back to Jackson. The response from the state was to securitize this prison and make it one of the most secure facilities in the state of Georgia.

Having put in extra razor wire, fencing and added gates, they now began to ship in prisoners who were some of the roughest in the state system. Habitual offenders, gang leaders, and inmates that could not be controlled or managed at other prisons were sent to Hays. Movement was controlled at all times, and men were marched in lines from the units to the gym, chow hall, visitation, or other programs. It became a paramilitary camp, and the harder they locked it down, the more violent it became. Fights were a normal occurrence, stabbings were almost daily, and gang fights broke out on a regular basis. One hundred and eighty beds were designated "the special segregation unit" and those cells remained full at all times. This is the prison where we would try our experiment. If it could work here, then it could work anywhere.

Actually, I had stumbled upon Hays quite by accident. I had seen a five-part National Geographic series entitled: *Hard Time: A Year inside Georgia's Toughest Maximum Security Prison*. I watched all five episodes and actually felt a calling to go and serve there. I cannot explain it other than it was ordained for me to do. Within weeks I had met someone who could make it happen and before I knew it, there I was. I began to meet these men who had the reputation of being the worst of the worst. But what I found was not at all what I expected. I found fathers, grandfathers, sons, brothers, uncles, and grandsons—just regular folks that were doing their best to survive, to just make it through another day. They were amazingly grateful, cheerful, and kind. Not all were like that of course. Many were hard, distant, and angry; many were indeed men to be very cautious and leery of. But my overwhelming feeling was that these men had just gotten off track and wanted somebody to come and see them. And I turned out to be that guy.

When I arrived at the prison the next week following my Philly Epiphany, I quickly went to see the warden. I excitedly told him about my idea and how it had come to me, to which he replied, "Have you lost your mind? This is a maximum security prison, son, and we are not ready for that." I did not blame him. Maybe it was a crazy idea. However, he did agree to allow me to teach the principles in my Tuesday class with the men in the Faith & Character program, and that's all I needed to hear. I had found my test group, and they would become the first initiates into the Power of Peace Project.

CHAPTER 2
WALKING A MILE WITH THE VICTIMS

I'm on my way to Grady Hospital in downtown Atlanta, and I'm speeding. It is seven in the morning, and I have just gotten a 911 phone call that will be a life changer. It's our son Justin, and he is in serious danger. Our son is a soldier, he had spent twelve years in the United States military, four combat tours in Iraq and Afghanistan, and is now back in the civilian world, successfully recovering from PTSD. He saw things and did things that the brain is not built to see and do. The effects of war live with him forever, and we are so grateful that he was able to make it through and begin rebuilding what was torn apart.

On this occasion he was home on leave from one of his tours and he and his wife were at a party downtown. There was a man at the party whom no one seemed to know. He was out of his head, probably on methamphetamine from the way he was behaving. He was acting errati-cally and being very disrespectful, almost in a rage. The turning point was when he actually slapped a girl right in front of everyone. That was the last straw. Instinct took over and Justin dealt with the situation. He took him outside and "handled" it. The guy left with his friends and it seemed as if it was over. A little while later the guy returned and began yelling out in the front yard. Hearing the commotion, Justin went back outside. A fight ensued and it looked as if the same thing would happen and they would run him off again. As they tangled, Justin became aware that the man had a knife. The man slashed wildly and by the time it was over Justin had been critically wounded: several deep cuts on his ribs and shoulder, but the most serious wound was all the way down his neck. His wife, who had also been stabbed as she tried to get the man off of Justin, came to his aid. Were it not for Justin's combat training, he would have most probably bled out. He told his wife two things that saved his life: keep pressure on the wound and do not wait for the ambulance. Three hours of surgery in a trauma unit, and with Justin being young and healthy, he would end up being OK— but have quite a scar and a story to carry around with him for the rest of his life.

That incident changed my life. You see, by this time I had grown very close to many convicts inside of Georgia's most violent and dangerous prison. Those men had taught me many things, and many of them protected me and even put their lives on the line for me. I had grown to love them and gotten close enough to them to understand what brought some of them to their worst day, the one that landed them where they are now. God had softened my heart toward people who had made the worst decisions and caused the most damage and wreckage. But there was a hole in my ministry: I did not understand what it was like to be on the other side of a violent crime, like so many families that we see on the news every day. These families are the innocent ones that are forever affected by the loss of a loved one, or a permanent disability, or years of trauma and therapy, financial ruin, wrecked relationships, constant fear, emotional illness, and a host of other horrible consequences of selfish, greedy, lustful, or hateful choices made by lost people. There is no way those things can ever be completely made right. It is very hard to understand someone else's pain until you have walked a mile in their shoes. Now, at least on some level, my wife and I were walking in those shoes. There was man out there who had tried, and almost succeeded, to murder our son—a war hero at that. He would eventually be picked up on another charge and convicted in this case, and serve four years in a Georgia state prison. Four years. We were not happy with this decision. Now that I was on the other side of the coin, I wanted the state to give him the most time the law allowed, to throw this young man away forever. It had become personal to us, but then again, every crime is personal to somebody.

The week that all of this happened, I made my way to the prison in North Georgia for my weekly visit. There is a fascinating connection that has been created between myself and convicts all over the country. I have found that I can be more open, vulnerable, and honest in these prisons than I can be anywhere else—even in churches. There is a lack of judgment and an understanding of pain, loss, and bad choices that allows for a powerful bond. So on this day I just opened up in front of a large group of hardcore, dangerous men and shared my heart about this situation. There was a heaviness and a still quietness that fell upon this room, a place where that is rarely the case. They were conflicted, because on one hand they cared deeply about me and my family, but on the other hand many of them were in there for doing the same thing that this man had done; but now it was more personal to them as well. They listened intently as I shared my pain, and even my tears, and some anger as well. Eventually a hand went up in the back of the room. I called his name and he asked the question that was on everyone's mind: "What's his name?" I asked for him to clarify. He said, "Tell us his name." Obviously this man was asking for me to identify the man for him so that they could find him when he got into the system. Then men began to nod and others began to say, "Just tell us his name." They said they wouldn't kill him, but just send him a message, and they told me that he would never hurt my people again. There is a very tight knit system in prisons across the country. Very few degrees of separation exist between one inmate and another. They can get to anyone at any time if properly motivated. I had become like family to them, and they have a unique way of taking care of their own. It was incredibly tempting for me to say his name. All I had to do was let it slip and I would have never heard about it again. The problem would have been taken care of and in some way it might have given me some relief, some revenge. But would that have truly solved anything?

Darkness cannot drive out darkness, and hate cannot drive out hate; only light and love can do that. I didn't give them the name, and somewhere out there was a convict that was healthy for the time being, but he had no idea how close he had come to a real problem. He is back in the free world now, but I doubt that he is truly free. I think about him from time to time, and I realize now that my heart has changed. Having the ability and the opportunity to hurt him, and choosing not to, had softened my heart toward this sick young man. Grace does that. Now I pray that I can meet him some day and teach him a better way. Maybe I can tell him this story and he can begin to understand grace as well. Mercy triumphs over judgment every time.

On some level, we are all victims, and we are all perpetrators. It is just a matter of degrees. I saw the darkness inside of me as I wanted vengeance. I also see the good inside of men that have done the seemingly unforgivable. There is light in all of us, and some darkness as well. On every side of a violent crime, two families lose. One family loses a loved one forever, and the other loses a loved one to the correctional system; a system that changes people forever. I have worked with mothers who have had a son or a daughter murdered, and I have worked with mothers who have had their son take a life and receive a life sentence. In both cases I see a family crushed and changed forever. And the cycle repeats.

The Redemption of Luis

My journey into this field began in 2009 as the result of a mother who was out of ideas and had exhausted all her resources. She had heard that I was working with people who found themselves in deep trouble, and she reached out to me hoping that I could help her son. I had known Luis when he was a kid, and he happened to be in a ministry that I was leading. We had hit it off, kind of like a big brother thing. But then I lost connection with him after I went to lead yet another church in another town, and now years later he was in big trouble as he faced a murder charge as a result of a gang-related altercation; not the first that he had seen. He had chosen that life and everything that came with it: running the streets, gone for days and sometimes weeks at a time, and worrying his mother sick. Now he was in a desperate situation, beaten into a state of reasonableness and ready for help, and I just happened to be there.

Because I knew Luis when he was a kid, I went into this county jail to see him that first night with no judgment or fear. I was just going to see a kid that I loved that was all grown up and needed my help. Over the next two years, after I had worked with Luis almost every week, I had seen him change and I developed a conviction: if a man is given the chance, and if he has someone to believe in him, then he can change—he only needs the desire. This prepared me to go and see all of the men I work with, and believe that all of them can change. Years later it continues to work, as hated, feared and forgotten men sense that I believe in them, with no preconceived notions, and they find hope, even if they have to borrow mine—hope that they too can change. Without Luis being ready, willing, and able to truly change, I would probably have never chosen to continue working with these fascinating, broken souls.

I had the unique perspective to see Luis from both sides: the victim and the perpetrator. I had known him when he was just a kid coming to church and looking for answers. He would wait in line to talk to me after my sermons and he always had something encouraging to say. He was always a little bigger than the other kids, but he had a charm and innocence that made him stand out. Things could have turned out so much differently for him. What if he'd by chance gone to another school? What if he had made friends with the kids that had chosen to bully him instead? What if he had fallen for a little girl that loved God? What if he would have had a coach or a teacher that paid him extra attention? So many variables that lead us to become the people we turn out to be. But it didn't go that way for Luis. He began hanging with the kids who didn't care much about school; they didn't respect authority; they didn't attract girls who respected themselves; they had way too much time on their hands; they wanted to be gangster, to be thug; and we become what we see, and we find those that are much like ourselves. We are the collective average of the five people who we spend the most time with. That can be a good thing, or a bad thing—a blessing or a curse.

Luis got initiated and quickly began moving up the food chain in this dangerous world. He had talent, brains, charisma, and tremendous courage. He was willing to do things that others weren't, and he was eager to make a name for himself. Over the years since I had seen him, he had become "somebody," but he had sacrificed so much in order to get there. When he walked out into the visitation room that night I didn't even recognize him. He was no longer a little boy. He was large, covered with tattoos, and his eyes, once big and brown, looked like they had died and gone dark. But he recognized me after all those years, and a smile came to his face. For a moment he softened, and came over and gave me a hug. We sat and talked for over an hour on that first night. I had no idea that my life had radically changed. Most significant turning points are like that, they come and go, and then one day we look back.

Over the next two years we began to educate one another: I gave him the tools to change and to begin to create a life that could lead to dreams and family and freedom, if even only from the inside. He taught me about the streets, gang life, crime and a dark world that I had never known. One day he made the choice not to fight, and took a beating instead. Luis actually laughed as they beat him. He did it not because he had to, but because he wanted to see if he could do it, to see how it felt. The men who had beat him down also took his possessions, only to return them the next day after they found out who he was. He had proven something not only to himself, but to me as well: tough and dangerous men can choose peace and most times they will if given the chance.

Over these past years since I reconnected with Luis, there has been so much that has happened between us. I've been in and out of court with him; been there when the attorney told us that he might be facing a death penalty, been there when his co-defendants stared me down in an open federal courtroom, been there when gang members threatened my life for talking to him, been there when police cruisers sat in our cul-de-sac because there was a credible threat, been there when I felt as though his family's lives were in danger, been there as he has been transferred from one facility to another and waited on a trial that has never come, been there as his mother waits and his kids grow older, been there when he felt as if I had abandoned him, been there...Luis will always be the beginning of this amazing story. As thousands of inmates and students take the 40 Day Challenge and sign the POPP Peace Pledge, they will never see Luis, sitting in a cell, having been the first to be brave enough to try it. I remember the day I baptized him, Cinco de Mayo 2010. An officer assisted on the other side of the glass, because I was considered a "high value hostage opportunity" in the facility where he was being held with other high profile gang members in this national case. I asked him if he were willing to die for his newfound faith and relationship with God. He looked at me and said, "All these years I've been willing to die for my gang, why would I not be willing to die for God?"

POPP and Attitude Science

You cannot give away something that you do not first possess, and I quickly realized that this better be a calling and not a career, and this was a life's work that one could not fake. This was going to be very uncomfortable and even painful in the beginning, because it was way outside my routine and comfort zone. I was going to call twelve men to literally put their lives on the line for peace, and I needed to design a program which would keep us motivated for forty days to do something that felt very unnatural, and could actually cause us bodily harm. I did not live there, but I was there twice a week and I understood that there were powerful men in that place that might not necessarily be fired up about men disrupting the system and possibly interfering with their ability to carry on business as usual. So I began to search for quotes from famous peacemakers and freedom fighters from the twentieth century.

These men and women had changed nations with non-violent principles, and I reasoned that the same could happen in this place. I believed that if these powerful principles were true, then they would work wherever and with whomever they were practiced. I just needed the space, access, and population with which to try them out. I came up with forty days of freedom fighter quotes from Gandhi, King, and Mandela. I would not reinvent the wheel, but rather borrow from movements that had already proven successful. I created action challenges for every one of the forty days that went along with the quotes for that day. This would develop momentum to the project, as well as give the men something new and fresh every day as they attempted to do something which had never been done in this dangerous community. But they needed more….

The deputy warden had asked if I could develop a program that would engage negative leaders and inmates who would not come to other faith-based and educational programs. She wanted the trouble-makers and the men who were running things, and she wanted to know if I could put together a program that would attract them. I told her that I had a program that I had created that was fairly effective in corporate events and schools, and that possibly I could adapt it to a prison population. It was entitled "Attitude Science," and I began to teach it to a group of inmates weekly. This became the platform from which we would launch all subsequent POPP programs. These are twelve timeless, universal laws and principles that I have picked up and implemented along the way. These have become my guideposts and my anchors when life gets challenging, or when I lose focus or fall off the beam. These foundational principles guide me and bring me back to center whenever I stray. I reasoned that they too would work for anyone, and what better place to experiment with the Attitude Science Project? This place became my field of dreams and we began to test these powerful principles:

1) I find what I look for
2) I find what I believe I deserve

3) I find that which is like myself

4) My thoughts become things

5) My words create my world

6) My moods are magnetic

7) What I focus on expands

8) What I resist persists

9) Passion resides in my unique gift

10) Joy often hides in my pain

11) What I seek is seeking me

12) All that I need I already possess

If I could get these twelve men to begin to see their world differently, then anything was possible. Week in and week out we would discuss these principles, and I would teach, share, and we would debate. We laughed, cried, and even argued—but we learned together and became a team. These men were hungry for change and they proved it with their actions. We began to see the potential that this new program held, but it was a work in progress and we were just getting started.

CHAPTER 3
FREE FALLING OVER GEORGIA

I'm looking down, outside the open door of a small plane over the North Georgia mountains. We are cruising at fourteen thousand five hundred feet above the planet. My heart is racing and pumping adrenaline, and it feels as though it will jump out of my chest. Everything inside is trying to get me to change my mind. But I've made a commitment and I can't back out now. My instructor Ted is literally on my back and he gives me a shove. We do a natural flip and then we begin our seventy second free fall, at one hundred and twenty miles an hour. My fear turns to pure exhilaration, as I've never felt so high and free in my life. I am trapped in the present moment and I am giggling with excitement and joy, as my body is now hit with a huge dopamine blast. Unbounded euphoria. And then the real fun begins…. When we reach the appointed height, Ted prepares me for a big jolt and then he pulls the rip cord, as he had done a thousand times before. My stomach comes up into my throat and I am now preparing for what I assume will be a smooth scenic ride over the rolling green hills below. Instead, we start spinning violently and Ted starts cussing like a sailor. Our first chute has failed, as it has gotten tangled up after it was deployed. As we spin wildly, he does something that I am not prepared for and would never have expected: he cuts away our chute, and then I watch it quickly fly away. Now we are in free fall once again, but we are at a much lower altitude than we are supposed to be at this point in our $259 adventure. Surprisingly, I am completely quiet, and my mind is eerily calm. I am trapped in space, and time seems to stand still. As I think about my short life, Ted is working feverishly to prepare to release our second chute, and the only one that we have left. He pulls the second cord and again we experience a big jolt. It works, unlike its predecessor, but it is smaller and faster than the first chute. Ted has the nerve to say, "Relax and enjoy the ride." When we finally hit the ground, I feel a tremendous release of emotion, as I have a huge sense of relief and gratitude. I am completely spent, but somewhat elated at the same time; exhausted, but wired. There is no small commotion as people begin running toward me asking if I am the "cut-away" guy, for they had seen the chute floating away without anyone strapped to it. I guess it is a big deal, and very long odds that it would happen on my first jump. A short few minutes of my life that I will never forget.

Everything began changing, and changing very quickly after that. I believe that it was the first step in dealing with my fear. My whole life had been controlled by psychological fear. Forcing my brain to do something that goes against every natural instinct and one of our two innate fears had unlocked something. My brain had blasted open new pathways and broken down boundaries and barriers. I had faced a big fear and stared it down. I had faced a worst case scenario and handled it bravely and without panicking. I have since learned that 99 percent of the things that we fear never come to pass—that is a true fact. Most of our fear is illusionary fear; fear that we have created out of worry, dread, doubt, or fantasy. Once we face our fears, we find out that many of them are paper tigers and impotent bullies that never have any real power over us that we do not willingly offer them. My life was changing.

The Drunken Fallen Preacher Comes Back to Life

Years earlier I had reached rock bottom at the age of forty. After a successful career as a preacher and church builder, I had just run out of gas. Married for fifteen years and a father of two beautiful children, for the first time in my life I experienced a full-blown burnout. It's not like I didn't see it coming, but I always thought I could just turn it around like I had done so many other times in my life. I always ended up on top, and my friends always felt as though I was the luckiest guy in the room. I had a knack for wiggling my way out of trouble, and good things just seemed to come to me. Whatever I tried came relatively easy for me, and I typically would rise to a leadership position whether it was school, sports or new professions. But this time was different, and it just kept getting worse. I was becoming more and more unhappy, and I began to think about quitting and moving on, more and more. I had responsibilities that kept me from walking away, but the way that I was living made my work unsustainable, and eventually everything just collapsed. Tired, disillusioned, and increasingly bitter, I resigned and walked away from once having led over two thousand people.

I grew up in an alcoholic household, and by the time I graduated college at the University of Georgia, I was the textbook adult child of an alcoholic. Beginning projects and rarely finishing them; racing out to the front ahead of my competition, only to become bored and move on to the next thing; charming and charismatic with an underlying manipulative insecurity. Plagued by an addictive personality of my own, I chased the next high and searched for an escape for the pain and pressures of life. But at the age of twenty-five I was thirsty for a change and experienced an authentic, sincere, and life-changing spiritual transformation. I embraced my new purpose in the same way I did everything else: with passion, enthusiasm and a vigorous work ethic. I quickly rose to the top and was put into leadership at a fast growing, non-denominational church. I moved up through the ranks, very excited about every promotion and the growing level of responsibility that each new position brought with it. I became very ambitious and developed a knack for growing the membership of a congregation, and became a type of specialist who could start a ministry, turn around a failing church, and increase the membership in a relatively short period of time. I loved the attention, and the validation that it fostered. I loved the adoration of the congregants and the praise I received. It filled in the gaps that were the product of my defects of character and my lack of emotional development. However, as I said before, it was unsustainable as my talent eventually over took and outran my character—and I fell hard.

It was a public fall, and many of my worst fears were realized. I was so concerned about what others thought, and for my precious, carefully constructed reputation, that when I fell, I experienced tremendous humiliation and despair. So I chose to run away, and go into a type of hiding; staying away from the people who knew me from my public life. Eventually I was living in an eight hundred square foot apartment, seeing my kids on the weekend and drinking heavily to try and stop the pain. I had lived for forty years in Atlanta and almost half of those were spent in a very public position. Lots of people knew me and I had become a "good story." You're not paranoid if everyone really is talking about you, and I became the subject of chatrooms and blogs among my former followers. I withdrew to dark, seedy places where I knew I wouldn't be recognized, and I believed that my best days were behind me. But then I experienced what alcoholics refer to as a moment of clarity. I decided that enough was enough and I went and got help, not knowing then that I was being prepared for the great work of my life. You see, now I understood pain, loss and suffering in a way that I had never known, and I could now relate to people who were at the end of their rope, and those who had made a complete mess of their lives. I had been truly humbled and learned the valuable lesson that it was not all about me. Broken and ready to serve, I set out to try to make a difference in the lives of the down and out, the least of these and the marginalized. When you have nothing to lose, you are in a position to do the greatest work of your life. You have faced your fears, seen the worst parts of yourself, and made some truly terrible choices, yet you remain—still standing. This is why I think the men in these tough prisons trust me. They can read people better than anyone, and they see deep down in me that I too have experienced pain and loss. This inner strength would become very valuable as I continued on in my work.

History of POPP and the Convict Code

One of the most challenging aspects of launching this new project was overcoming the prevailing thought and belief system inside of this dysfunctional community. Much like the discriminatory South during the Civil Rights Movement, or apartheid in South Africa, the correctional complex in this country is a broken system that is not working, but many of those in charge do not have sufficient motivation to change it. Corrections is very effective at locking offenders up and keeping them away from the general public, which is important. The current system is also very effective at locking inmates down during their incarceration depending on security and threat levels, which is also very important. Our system has not proven effective, however, at rehabilitating those arrested and preparing them to reenter society in a condition in which they are not likely to reoffend. Something has to be done, because 97 percent of the 2.4 million incarcerated in the land of the free are coming home one day. The question is what condition will they come home in and how will they function in our communities, where our families live, work and worship? So if those in charge cannot or will not change it, then it is left to those within the system to change it for themselves, again very much like those caught up in the Civil Rights Movement in the South. If things were going to change, they were the ones who were going to have to create the shift.

There is also a system at work on the "inside" of these institutions which lies at the core of the problem. It is called the convict code. This code is effective in running this world that most people never see. It is the way that a new resident must learn to operate in these facilities in order to survive and create some sort of reasonable existence as long as he must live in that place. These are the rules of the game, how things work, and the way the players operate. It is all based on respect, reputation, and credibility. Inmates learn very quickly how to carry themselves and what to do and not do in order to get what they need, stay out of trouble and handle trouble when it finds them. This is a place where there is no alone time, and you cannot simply "mind your own business." Your business is everybody's business and a code has developed, although very dysfunctional, which allows some sort of normalcy to emerge. It is not a matter of whether you are going to live by the code or not, but rather how quickly you learn it and how well you can operate within it. The strong are feared and the weak are dominated. Everything works around fear, domination, manipulation, and control. This is why one third go into the system having been convicted of non-violent offenses, but two thirds come out having learned how to live violently while inside. The recidivism rate continues to climb, and many times sick and angry men are released back to our communities. The code has to be changed, but I could not launch this new program by pretending that it did not exist.

For decades I have been fascinated with the Civil Rights Movement. Born and raised in Atlanta, Georgia, I grew up in the Bible Belt, right in the heart of the segregated South. I was born in 1964 which was a very significant year in the turbulent sixties: Dr. King won the Nobel Peace Prize and the Civil Rights Act of 1964 was signed into legislation; Mr. Mandela went to Robben Island and began his twenty-seven year incarceration and long walk to freedom; Malcolm X made his life-changing pilgrimage to Mecca; Bob Marley released his first single and the Beatles came to America. The nation watched in horror as protestors were hit with fire hoses, attacked by police dogs, beaten on the streets, simply because they wanted equal rights. The system in place was wrong, and someone needed to take a stand. Dr. King was leading a nonviolent struggle while many of his contemporaries were urging blacks to fight back and meet force with force, and violence with more violence. It was Martin who said, "You cannot drive out darkness with darkness; only light can do that. You cannot drive out hate with hate; only love can do that." He changed the system from the inside out, but it was the oppressed that led the charge and they suffered for righteousness, until they eventually aroused the conscience of a nation.

For years now I have been teaching and exhorting convicts across the country that if the system is broken and needs to change, they are the only ones who can change it. In the same way that the powers that be were not going to simply change the system just because those that were suffering demanded it, the current problems in our justice and correctional systems are not going to change overnight just because it isn't working for some. However, we are reaching a stage in our nation's history that is unparalleled. The prisons are overflowing and we can't build them quickly enough. The inmates are getting younger and younger, going away for longer time, for lesser crimes. Men are getting out hungrier, angrier and more violent than when they went in, and they are becoming increasingly more dangerous—and they are being released to go back to *our* communities. In what condition will they return? Governors, senators, congressmen, commissioners, and police chiefs are having to get ever more serious about this problem, and more solution-minded, because just getting tougher and tougher on crime is not solving the problem.

I believe that convicts themselves are going to have to choose to start living more peacefully with one another. They can't wait for the "other side" to change first because that will never happen. In order to get more programs, education and treatment into the prisons so that inmates can get the cure to what is really ailing them, we must first have more peace. Prisons and administration are never going to allow more movement, freedom, access and volunteers in an increasingly violent environment— that would not be doing their jobs, which is to protect the public, their staff, and the inmates under their charge. So we need a program, a project, better yet, a movement, which creates a more peaceful environment so that faith-based programs and treatment oriented education can be brought in and allowed to thrive. In general, programs are effective in helping inmates to get out and become less likely to reoffend. The problem is that we can't get enough inmates to get involved in those programs or at least not the ones who need it, because they are busy worrying about basic survival. The Power of Peace Project does not claim to be the end-all and be-all solution, but we are proving that POPP brings about more peace and less violence so that the programs already in place can flourish and get the help to the men and women who truly need it.

CHAPTER 4

THE HAYS EXPERIMENT

I'm sitting in the audience at Georgia's roughest state prison. I'm surrounded by men in white with a blue stripe. This is the standard issued uniform in the Georgia Department of Corrections. I am naïve as to my surroundings. I do not know what a state prison should be like, for this is the first time that I have ever been in one. I do not yet know that this is the toughest prison in the state. I do not know that this is the prison with the most active gang members. I do not know that a third of the men are doing life sentences, and another third are classified as "mental health cases." I do not know that the word is out throughout the sixty thousand convicts in the system in Georgia that you do not want to come here, and there is a fear present that no one sees inside of every man that gets off the bus into this place. It has a reputation, a unique energy, and an intense vibe. But I do not know what I do not know, and that turns out to be an advantage for me here.

A man sits next to me that goes by the nickname "SB." In here everyone has a nickname. We begin to talk and we hit it off. For some reason it does not occur to me to judge him. I don't wonder what he did, or fear him, or even worry about whether I could trust him. For some strange reason all of that is gone. I just see HIM. He is strong, very intelligent, cool, and a good communicator. I can tell that he is "somebody" in there by the way that other inmates treat him.

We made a connection that first day and it would be one that would last. He began to teach me things about living life inside a maximum security prison. I became a student of things I couldn't have learned any other way. He taught me how a man needs to carry himself in there, how to take care of yourself, how to get the things you need, and how to keep from owing anybody. He taught me how he learned to defend himself; how to look a man in the eye, and how not to look; and how to survive in a place where nobody wants to be. He taught me how to be respected without necessarily getting connected. He taught me how important trust is, and how dangerous it can be in a place like that. He taught me many things that I carry with me to this day. So much of that early training from my first friend on the "inside" would prepare me to be who I needed to be as I began to work in more dangerous environments.

On this day SB is a little down, and a little more on edge than normal. He says, "It's been out of control up here lately, bro. We've had nineteen stabbings in the last twelve days." The reality of where he lives hits me. I think it registers on my face, because then he says, "But you don't have to worry man—two things you gotta know: One—we got a code in here. Ain't nothin' gonna happen to a guy like you. And two—if anybody does try to get at you…" Then he becomes very serious, "You got people in here that will die for you bro."

I didn't know it fully then, but I would later learn that he meant it. For possibly the first time in my life, I had someone outside of my own family that would lay down his life for me, and he just happened to be a convict. A band of brothers were emerging in a dark and hopeless place.

Andre's Emergence

Andre had been in the front row of our earlier "Attitude Science" group that initially met on Tuesdays in the Y Building at Hays. This was a group of young men: white, black and Latino. They ranged from seventeen to thirty years old and most of them were doing life sentences, and some were gang affiliated. Dre, as they called him, was quiet and serious, and intense. He was twenty-seven, connected, and two years into a thirty year life sentence. His skin was very light, and although he was black, they also called him "White Boy." He had considerable influence, and he was trying to change his life, but still very much a part of his organization. It turned out that he was literally waiting for somebody to call him to do something great. He was, and always will be, the first convict to sign the Peace Pledge—his name is at the top of that document. He took the challenge very seriously, and he began to use his influence and spread the word. Soon he was bringing powerful guys from various gangs to meet me and begin talks about the prison peace movement. His impact was immediate and obvious and will forever be a major part of the Power of Peace history.

It was a decision that he made on his own that created the first significant shift. He lived in the only dorm that had air conditioning. It was where the faith and character program was housed and carried special privileges. Once Dre had taken hold of the Peace Project, he no longer wanted to stay in the most comfortable housing unit with the model inmates. He didn't feel as though he was needed as much back there as he was in the general population, for that was where the violence was happening and where peace was needed most. So he went to the warden and asked if he could be relocated to C-1. It was situated right in the middle of the compound and was one of the toughest dorms in the institution. So he packed his stuff and moved back to "Gen-Pop." He was known and he had a reputation. So when he got back into the C Building there were certain expectations of him and pressures and temptations to deal with. However, he was highly motivated because he had found a great purpose, even in a place like this—as a matter of fact—especially in a place like this.

When he got up early his first morning back in C-1, his first move was to get a bucket, soapy water and a big brush. He got on his hands and knees in front of God and everybody and began cleaning the common area. As more and more inmates got up and noticed what he was doing, many were surprised, others were confused, and many made fun of him. They said, "What's the matter with you Dre, you don't have to do that? What's up man, have you gone soft?" He ignored them and continued scrubbing saying, "If a man can't respect the place he lives, then he won't ever respect himself." After almost a week of this, the very first thing every morning, finally a group of young thugs came up to him. He didn't know what they intended. One spoke up and said, "Give us the bucket and the brush, Dre. We're gonna clean for you today. You go get some rest." That one move eventually led to evening prayer meetings for the dorm, a peace box with donated honey buns for those who could not afford them, along with a new unit reputation as peace came to C-1. They began to call it the POPP dorm and it became the model dorm on the compound. He had shared his purpose with them, and they began to take pride in where they lived.

Several months later there was a stabbing in C-1 and the consequence of that event was that their TV was taken away. Andre took the incident very seriously, and personally. That could not be tolerated in the Peace Dorm. There was a standard that had been developed and they no longer allowed for knuckleheads to disturb the fragile new peace. The following Friday we had our open call out "Peace at Hays" meeting for everyone who was serious about peace or curious about the movement. That day the room was packed, as we had the biggest crowd to date. There were very influential, rival convicts in the room and the energy was high. In those early days I would have Dre open the meeting, give a few remarks, and then introduce me for that day's message. He is a great speaker and he commanded a very rare respect from inmates, speaking to an audience of dangerous men.

Without my knowledge, Dre had invited the warden to attend the meeting that day. He regularly dropped by to look in, and every now and then he would have some words of encouragement for the men. But this day he was personally invited to be in attendance. As Andre got up to speak, he addressed the warden directly. I was surprised and immediately concerned. I did not know what he was up to. In front of all the men he said, "Warden, the men of C-1 have a special message for you." Then he looked at the audience and said, "All the brothers in C-1 stand up." As one, all the inmates from the POPP dorm stood at attention, about thirty-five in number. It was powerful and impressive, and something that never happened in a prison like this. He continued, "We would like to apologize for the stabbing that happened in our building earlier this week, and we are going to commit to you that we will not let it happen again. It is unacceptable and we will not tolerate it." Then he turned back to the men and said, "You can be seated." And they all sat down at once. The warden acknowledged what he had said and turned and left the room.

I knew I was in trouble. I walked up to Andre at the end of the meeting and said, "Wherever they transfer you, I will come and see you." He looked confused. "You will be transferred soon, they will see to that," I said. He was shipped out the following week. He had become too powerful and he had to go. He would later write to me and apologize to me sincerely. He saw his personal ambition and pride and told me he had grown from it. I later learned that he had gotten busy at his new prison right away, and began to establish the prison peace movement there as well. I had learned a valuable lesson too: do not give the inmates too much authority and influence, for it can undermine administrative leadership and end up hurting them as well. I never made that mistake again.

The POPP Process: Part One—the Pledge and the Four Anchors

I operate under the conviction that inside of every one of us there lies the desire to do something extraordinary. Each of us therefore carries the need to be challenged to do something great, and when we are called to do our great work, something inside of us wakes up and comes alive. That is what I did with the twelve: I challenged them to do something great. They were there all those years just waiting. Andre had longed for someone to see him, believe in him, and call him to do something truly great with his life. As soon as I challenged them, something woke up and came alive in the group. A different energy developed and a momentum began, and we were off and running. After that it was more about harnessing and directing that powerful energy. At times it lulled and needed to be renewed. Other times it got misdirected and needed to be brought back on track. But it was a living thing now, this collective purpose and passion.

The pledge was a significant development for this young peace movement. It was a moment where they could witness one another's commitment to change, make their own public declaration, make themselves accountable, and take responsibility for their actions and choices. It was empowering, it was liberating, and it was unifying. The twelve original inmates signed a seven-point peace pledge on Jan 18, 2011, and since then thousands of convicts and students have followed their lead. We would look back at the day that they collectively signed and remind them of when, where, and why they had signed. We would remind each other of why we had taken a stand when we began to stray. It kept us clear as to what our strategy was and our mission remained in focus. Today it has become the cornerstone of the Power of Peace Project. I tell the story of the twelve and call men to follow their example of nonviolence. We would challenge one another and share every week about our struggles, failures, and victories as we tried to live nonviolently in a place where the world says that it cannot happen.

Accountability works when we have someone who supports our vision, has our best interests at heart, and is there for us when we need encouragement, guidance, and support. However, accountability only works when we want to change. This group desperately wanted to change their environment. They were sick and tired of having to live the way that they were living and they wanted to do easier time. This led to the development of the four POPP anchors. The potential initiates are asked a series of four questions that will become "agreements" as we move through the 40 Day Project:

1) Raise your hand if you want to do hard time.
2) Raise your hand if you have family back home that you want to return to.
3) Raise your hand if you can sense when something is about to happen in this community before it does.
4) Raise your hand if you believe that you have the power, collectively, to prevent or avoid a violent situation when you become aware that it is about to happen.

These four questions create a very heavy energy in the room. None of them want to do hard time; if given the choice every man will choose easy time, because we were all created to live in peace, and inside of every one of us is the desire to have peace. None of them wish suffering on their families and they do not want their kids to follow their former example and end up living there as well. This appeals to their need to be good fathers, as they were created to be. They believe they run things, that they know when things are going to happen before they do, and that they possess the power to change things. Then they are reminded that they were created to live in community and that they are a tight knit group, however dysfunctional they might be. The logical conclusion is that they can use their influence for peace in order to create easy time, learn to be good parents and role models, and begin to decrease violence and conflict in their community. Then I challenge them man to man: "If you say those things are true, and you are still living in a way that brings violence to this community, then you are full of crap. Period." They can't believe I've just said it, but they agree with it and we can move on. They just need a purpose and the motivation to begin—and then they get hooked on peace in the process.

In all the prisons where I've asked these four questions, not one hand has gone up when I asked if they wanted to do hard time. There is not one man, no matter how far gone, sick, wounded or twisted, who wants to have to watch his back all the time, take a weapon to the shower, or live in hatred and fear—not one. Not one hand has ever gone up when I've asked if they want their sons or little brothers to come there. With all the dysfunctional, broken, and toxic family relationships out there, not one man has ever been so hateful that he wanted his family to suffer, for it goes against the natural order of things. We can build on that, and that is where we begin. The other powerful point in this part of the process is that they have all just agreed that they have families out there in the free world that they love, that they care about their kids and little brothers, and that they all want to live in peace. That is commonality that we can build on. For just a moment they have admitted publicly that they share some very sacred things in common. Instead of focusing on all the things which separate us, we will take forty days and focus on the things we have in common.

CHAPTER 5

TELL THE PEACEMAKER TO WATCH HIS BACK

It's Friday morning and men are coming through the security check point into our meeting room. There is no metal detector in this area and there are never any guards present during our open call out in this maximum security prison. We have found that we have a more powerful, authentic, and effective meeting if there are no keys "jangling" in the back of the room. The men that are coming in are some of the more powerful and influential men on this compound; we have planned it that way. These are leaders or high ranking members of some of the larger organizations in this very notorious prison. However, there is a lighter energy in this room on Friday mornings than you would normally find among this group. Many of these men are rivals, and typically wouldn't or shouldn't share the same space with one another. But on Fridays they enjoy coming to this gathering to experience a little laughter, hope, and sometimes even a few goose bumps. They put aside their differences, if only for a moment, and dream together. But this is still a maximum security prison, and these are still dangerous, high risk inmates that do not get along—so anything is possible at any given moment.

Today I have asked a couple of the leaders to share the mic after I speak. One of the men whom I have grown to respect is a man they call "Dae Dae." He is serving four life sentences and he has been a warrior for many of the years that he has been down. When there is a gang war, he is the guy they turn to. Everyone knows his name and he rarely if ever attends meetings, and when he does come he doesn't speak. But he has come to respect this movement and he desperately wants change, so he not only agrees to come but also to speak. He tells me he has something to say. I brief him on the ground rules: only constructive conversation, no talk of gangs or specific organizations, no singling out other convicts, and no criticism of staff or administration. He agrees and we start the meeting.

My message on peace and reconciliation is well received, and then I invite Dae Dae to the podium. As he walks up, it becomes very quiet and still. No one knows what he is about to say, and neither do I. He pauses for what seems like a long time. He clears his throat, and fumbles over his words. Then he says: "I am tired. I'm just really tired. I've got four life sentences and I am never going home. I never wanted to do this, and I never wanted to be here. I have a woman that I love that I can never go home and see. All I want is love. I've become something I never wanted to be." His voice cracks and tears begin to fill his eyes. He is breaking all the rules of the convict code and doing what everyone believes you should never do in there. He is not crying or weeping, but just letting some bottled up emotion spill over.

Sitting on the front row is a man named Miami. Miami has been down for thirty-one years. He too is a warrior. He speaks up even less than Dae Dae does. He has learned how to do hard time, and he is never going home. His "family" happens to be a rival organization of Dae Dae's. As Dae Dae shares his heart, Miami stands up and starts toward the podium. All eyes now turn toward Miami as no one knows why he has gotten up without being invited, and neither do I. Dae Dae turns to face him as Miami reaches into his pocket. Now, everybody knows that there are weapons present, though unseen, at this particular meeting. No one is going to admit it, and I can't go on record and say that this is the case, but the kind of men that are in this room and the number of opposing groups? Everyone knows that certain men from every group have brought "tools" to the meeting. So when Miami reaches into his pocket everyone is wondering what will happen next. He pulls out a tissue. That's right, a tissue. He stretches out his hand, and in one powerful gesture, he sends a message to the whole group: we are all in this together. Dae Dae accepts the gift and wipes his face. They give one another the "convict hug" and both go and sit down.

Right around this same time I received a heads up from one of the brothers at Hays. It came in the form of something called a "kite." A kite is an important means of communication in the prison system, because they are not supposed to have cell phones and there are heavy penalties if you get caught with one. They have no email, text messaging, social media, or phone calls. They rely on a fascinating communication system of very small notes written in sometimes microscopic hand writing and these get passed along by some very creative methods. Information can be passed, instructions communicated, rumors circulated, orders given, or questions asked. Requests can be submitted to administration this way, but mainly it is a way that convicts stay connected through a tight knit sub-culture while flying under the radar. One day a message from a kite was passed along to someone that was close to me. He came to me and hesitantly delivered the message. It simply read, "Tell the white boy to watch his back." During this time at this dangerous prison, with all that was going on there, it was very obvious who the particular person was that this kite was referring to. There was someone out there that was telling me that I had to be careful, and that obviously there were men inside that prison that were not happy about the work we were doing, and the way it was affecting their ability to carry on business. I began to pay closer attention while getting more connected to the power brokers in this dark facility—things were changing and the waters were being disturbed.

Sir Brown's Protection and Influence

I never felt like I needed protection in that place, but the recent threat had gotten my attention. After Andre got shipped to another prison, it created a vacuum of leadership. We needed a new leader and I needed someone who could help me be smart, stay safe, and continue to keep my finger on the pulse of this young movement. One man had set himself apart from the rest. Raised in a tough neighborhood in Jersey, Sir Brown, as they called him, was strong, street wise and good with his hands. On the streets he had a reputation for robbing drug dealers, so he also feared no man. His adopted father was a local hood legend who spent the last forty years preaching in storefront churches, and he would go and find Brown from time to time in abandoned houses and give him a place to sleep, a shower, and a good meal. Brown grew to love this man and he is his hero to this day. Brown earned great respect in this maximum security prison, even though he never joined a gang or relied on any organization for protection. Gang leaders would constantly come to him for advice and counsel and he was already using his influence for peace when we first met; he just needed a cause and for someone to call him to do something great where he was. Many plan on doing things right when they get out, but that is an illusion. If you don't practice today what you want to be tomorrow, then you'll be the same again day after day. Wherever you go, there you are.

As the peace movement began to develop at Hays, Brown would come to the meetings and always sit on the front row. He promised me that nothing would ever happen to me when he was present. He became a trusted friend, advisor, ally, and bodyguard to me, though I never expected or asked for it. Since then he has become one of the men in this world that I trust with my life and who I love deeply. He became the inmate leader of this young peace movement and kept it moving after the prison was locked down. To this day he continues to bring peaceful resolution to conflict and teach young brothers a better way. He educates young and old convicts and helps them learn to read and get their GEDs.

I will always be grateful for his partnership and friendship, and he'll never truly know how instrumental he has been in shaping and developing what is becoming a national peace movement for young people. And I'll never know how many times he protected me from potential harm or danger, or maybe even saved my life—for he would never tell me. One time he was held back from the call out one Friday morning. He couldn't make it to the Peace at Hays meeting so we had to go on without him. Later when he caught me in the yard, he looked at me sternly and said, "I don't ever want you to have that meeting without me there. If anything ever happened to you I wouldn't be able to live with myself. If I'm not there then something is wrong, just send for me, because I will always be there for you." I was speechless.

Fifteen Dorms in the Heat

I reached a point where I began to realize that we were going to have to be more deliberate and aggressive in our strategy. If we couldn't get to the guys who were running things from behind the scenes, then our impact would be very limited. So I made a radical decision, and one that Brown considered before he advised me to move on it. After getting approval from the warden, I scheduled a "tour" through the fifteen dorms in this facility, which was still the number one gang prison in the state. Lately there had been considerable gang violence, and for the first time I was going into their living quarters; a place that they typically do not allow free world volunteers to go, especially when the vibe was the way it was then. The plan was for me to spend fifteen minutes in each dorm and deliver my message and challenge them to join the peace initiative. It would take me approximately three hours in 100 degree heat to get in front of about 1,200 inmates. This was on a Friday morning, which happened to be the only day of the week that the inmates don't have early morning inspection and they can sleep in. For me to be able to speak to them all at once in each unit we would have to turn off their big electric fan, and I would have to call them away from their bunks, TV, showers, or card tables. None of these things would be very popular, and no one was even aware that I was coming. On top of that there was someone out there, or more than one, who had made a threat toward me, and I had no idea who or which dorm they were in.

To begin each of the short messages, I shouted at the top of my lungs, "Dr. King said…" and heads would turn. It would get quiet and men would look out of their open cell door to see who was shouting. Men who had their backs turned at the tables in the open area turned around and faced me. Convicts came out of the showers and some sat on the stairs and on the top tier to listen. I was amazed at the respect that Dr. King carried in this place. I would lead up to the challenge and end with, "If you were twenty one years old in 1965, and Dr. King called you to march with him, would you have had the balls to march non-violently, or would you have joined the angry mobs to loot and riot? True courage is non-violent, and violence is cowardly." I left behind a blank sheet with numbered spaces, and challenged them to sign up for the prison peace movement. In some dorms they clapped when I finished. In others they stared and remained quiet. In some dorms I was heckled and warned. At one point during one of my stops, a man walked right up behind me and whispered into my ear while I preached, "You better get that shit out of here, white boy." I continued and trusted that God was in control. By the time I was done, I was exhausted and drenched with sweat. At the end of the day there were three hundred and fifty men who had signed up to take a stand for peace. The movement was gathering momentum at Hays.

CHAPTER 6

SCALING DOWN A HIGH-RISE FOR HOPE

I'm standing on top of a high rise building in downtown Atlanta. The view is gorgeous. It's a beautiful fall day, clear and sunny, about 70 degrees. Everything is just right, except for one thing: I've never rappelled before. They had promised that there would be training involved. That five minute lesson didn't feel like training. Once again this "I go wherever I'm invited" thing has gotten me out on a ledge. This time it is for another good cause: teenage addiction, overdose, and suicide. How could I say no? This event is called Shatterproof and it is the result of a family's worst nightmare. A young man had overdosed and died as a result of heroin addiction and this was the heroic response of a grieving family—to start a non-profit to save other families from their worst day. They go to big cities and find a high rise to scale and issue the "Shatterproof Challenge" and get people to climb down a building for a good cause. So here we go…. I am hooked up to equipment that I have never worn, and about to attempt something that I have never practiced, or ever even tried. The building looked big from the ground, but from this vantage point it looks monstrous—twenty-two stories. I can look over the Atlanta skyline and the crowd at the bottom of the building looks like ants. There is a radio station sponsoring the event and local CBS and FOX have crews filming. There are people cheering, kids playing and loud music blaring. They tell me it is my turn, and they invite me to step up onto the ledge. "Just lean back," the expert says. Just lean back, yeah right.

The big WHY can make people do some crazy things. Many of the men I try to help just had the wrong why: money, a woman, a drug, revenge, reputation, etc. All of those are strong enough to push you beyond normal limits, but if you add a noble inspiration and a worthy cause? Practically nothing can stop you; it will move you through pain, fear, doubt, worry, and even consequence. And this "Big Why" was driving me: we've got to let the world know that we are losing our kids. So I step back over the edge and cautiously lean back. The instructor gives very important directives: "Trust your tools, listen to my voice, don't try to go too fast, and if you get stuck just give me the sign, and I will un-stick you." I begin my descent and fear turns to focus. Once again I was trapped in the powerful present moment. I wasn't thinking about what I had done the day before or what I had on my schedule tomorrow. Just one thing mattered: handle the task at hand. I was doing fine until I reached the mid-way point. You see there is a safety catch which will grab and lock you if you are going too fast, and once it locks you need help from above. Well, I got stuck. I was trusting the tools, listening to the voice on my walkie-talkie, and I was trying to go smooth and steady—but I still got stuck. There I was hanging by a rope from a tall building, stuck, in front of God and everybody. Then I remembered the "sign." I was told just to throw my hands out to my side and look up—that was the help sign. That was easy at this point because I could not unstick myself. Why do we have such a hard time asking for help when we get stuck? So many of us could save ourselves and those who love us so much heartache and pain if we would just throw our hands out and look up for help—but many of us don't.

Motivation is so important in life—your big WHY. The teens in trouble got me on top of this building, but there was more that would end up getting me down it. At the base of this big building was my little three year old grandson Jesco. The whole time that I was coming down, I could hear a tiny voice shouting "Papa, Papa, Papa." That small voice encouraged me when I got stuck, and I kept on climbing down. But there was more that was driving me from a very deep place on this day. My dad died in 1988 from this disease of addiction. He died before I was ever able to say that I was sorry. I never had the chance to tell him that I forgave him. He never got to see me change and become the man I am today. He was gone at fifty-two, way too young, and I was busted up for a long time—part of me just broke and went dark. For years I would speak publicly and write and share about our dysfunctional relationship. I would heal by preaching and teaching about the pain. It was cathartic, but it didn't completely heal the wound. I believe that the one who can best heal the wound is the one who created it. But he was gone and we weren't able to fix it.

When I committed to rappelling down this high rise they asked who I would be climbing in honor of. I told them Johnny Howard Cummings, my father who died in 1988. I didn't really understand how the whole thing would work and why they had asked. As I climbed down the sky scraper, the music stopped and the DJ began to speak, blasting a message out for the whole world to hear: "Ladies and gentlemen, Kit is rappelling today in honor of his father Johnny Cummings, who he lost at the age of fifty-two in 1988." Here I was twenty-seven years later honoring him in front of a cheering crowd, and his name was literally being shouted from the rooftops. Quite fitting. The wound was finally being healed and I believe that he walked with me all the way down that "mountain."

All those years since my father's death, I had never felt very close to him and tended to remember only the negative aspects of our dysfunctional relationship. However, one night he came to me in a lucid dream, which was something I had never experienced before. I rarely dreamed of him, and I cannot remember any other significant dreams regarding my dad. This was an experience that was so clear, and so vivid, that I can see it now as I recall it. I was still heart stricken from our fractured relationship and the abrupt way that it had ended. He was so old looking when he passed and I never got to say goodbye. I never had gotten over the fact that we didn't get our problems resolved, and that he never got to meet my children or my wife, or hear me preach. He stood there in my dream and he was beautiful. It was my father on his very best day. He looked about thirty years old, and he was happy, healthy, and strong. His eyes were clear and he was smiling brightly. He had a message for me. He said, "Son, I'm proud of you, and I wanted you to know that I am alright. I love you." And then he was gone. I had received what I needed after all that time. My heart was being healed, and the light was emerging. Maybe rappelling was a step in the right direction for the whole family, because addiction is a family disease. My sister Lisa has come through a lot over the years as well. I am so proud of her, as she has spent an entire career using her God-given talents, gifts, and fine-tuned skills to try to keep the world safe from evil threats abroad. In our own different ways, we are both trying to save the world. She is brilliant, and I know my dad is proud of her as well. I will be going to spend time with her in India soon as I explore the land of Gandhi and Mother Teresa. I can't wait.

But I know this for a fact: I would never have even had the chance to experience my healing without the love of a mother who would never even consider giving up on me. I don't know anyone else who can say that they have never been at odds with their mama, but that is my truth as far as I know it. I have put her through a lot in my time on this planet, but I honestly cannot remember a time in my life when we were not close. She has walked with me through the darkness, carried me through the fire, fiercely protected me when no one else would, and forgiven me more times than what seemed acceptable. She is my friend, my advocate, my counselor, my teacher, my adviser and my confidant. I could not even imagine this journey without her and I hope to take care of her as she has taken care of me. We have come through it all protecting one another, and that is the way it will always be. A true mother in every sense of the word.

Hurting People Hurt People

Every one of the men and women that I work with have been wounded, and hurting people hurt people. They are fathers and mothers; sons and daughters; grandfathers and grandchildren. They are typically poor, but not always. They are largely a product of addiction or abuse, although some of them just had a bad day. They were driven to their worst day by desperation, passion, poverty, retaliation, or extreme pressure. But every one of them have a very compelling story of what got them where they are in life; where you end up has a lot to do with where you begin. It is much easier to judge at a distance than up close and personal. Hatred happens at a distance but the closer I get to a person, the more I start to see similarities and commonality rather than what separates us. When I walk a mile with a man, I begin to see clearly that if given the same opportunities, challenges, struggles and influences, then I might very well of chosen his exact same path. In the same way that no one can truly know what it is like to live my life, how in the world can I presume to know another's?

These are men who have been hurt and caused much damage, and are living in a place where they have become accustomed to hurting one another simply because of their differences. So it is crucial to help them begin to find the things that they have in common rather than what separates them. One of the scenarios that we present to the prisoners is the following. Imagine if we took all of the men in a particular prison and put them on a plane, and all of them wearing their prison issued uniforms. Let's say we drop them off in a hostile country where Westerners are hated and feared. Then they are told to fend for themselves and to figure out a way to survive in a very treacherous land, as the plane takes off and flies away, leaving them in grave danger. Very quickly they would be forced to seek out the things they had in common with one another. It wouldn't matter if one was from the west side of Detroit and the other was from the east side. It wouldn't matter if one were black and the other white, or one was Christian and the other Muslim. It suddenly would not matter if one were Crip and the other Blood, or one was "Thirteens" and the other

"Eighteenth Street." What would matter is that they were all from the same country and in danger and that they'd better all stick together. Then I tell them, "You can choose to stick together now, because you all happen to be wearing the same clothes and are being forced to live together for a while. Why not create easier time and a better quality of life for yourselves?" If pushed, they will admit that by and large they DO have the power to make that change. Then let it be so, now.

The Origin of the POPP Steps

Addiction and violence oftentimes stem from pain and woundedness. Hurting people hurt other people—and themselves as well. Step programs work, and those who work them honestly and diligently experience change. I now see clearly that if my father would have gotten into twelve step recovery, he would have had a chance to get sober and heal his wounded relationships. He was a good man, but he was hurting deeply and the pain of those wounds were sometimes taken out on the people who he loved the most.

Step programs are effective because like-minded people meet together regularly and commit to a well-defined process. I went to my first twelve step group when I was twenty years old, and I began to lay the foundation of a life of long-term recovery. When I lost my dad to the disease of alcoholism in 1988, my life took a dark turn for a season. I struggled with my genetic tendencies off and on for the next twenty years. At the age of forty, I went back to a twelve step program that saved my life and helped my dreams come true. There is power in the steps. It's not necessarily the steps that are magical in and of themselves, but rather it is the process of surrendering your will to a proven set of timeless laws and universal principles. When a group of individuals come together for a common purpose, then magic happens. That is how and why we developed the seven step programs which are the foundation of the Power of Peace Project.

I was searching for a way to bring these prisoners together for forty days and give them a way to keep them focused, hold one another accountable, and stay on track. I was very familiar with the method and effectiveness of twelve step recovery, so I just implemented what had worked for me by creating seven steps around non-violent principles that had worked for peacemakers from the twentieth century. These men would help me prove that peace is not only possible, but it is promised to those who voluntarily choose to live by these powerful steps for just forty days at a time. The promises are what keep you moving when things get tough and you find obstacles in your way. The steps become daily commitments and anchors to hold you steady when the storms of temptation come.

The POPP Steps: 40 Days to Freedom

1) I will seek first to understand my opponent
2) I will find common ground with my adversary
3) I will walk a mile in the other man's shoes before I judge him
4) I will actively listen and pause before responding
5) I will deliberately communicate and use my influence for peace
6) When wrong, I will promptly admit it and quickly make amends
7) I will treat my enemies with dignity and respect even when we disagree

I understood that before I could challenge them to choose nonviolence in a maximum security prison, first we had to begin to relate to one another. These steps began to put each one of them in the other man's shoes. These men have been beefing for so long that they don't even know or remember why they hated each other. All of them have moms that they love. All of them believe in something bigger than themselves. And they all have made terrible mistakes and choices which most of them deeply regret. That would be the beginning of their journey together: they would commit to trying to see things from the other man's point of view, for just forty days. It was a start.

A Shift toward Youth

I recently had the chance to speak to an amazing group of young men, but they were quite possibly the most challenging audience I have ever faced—and that says a lot. I was asked to come to Circleville Juvenile Correctional Facility in Ohio because of a rise in violence there due to youth gang recruitment, attacks and retaliation. I go where I am invited, so I quickly made plans to launch 40 Days to Freedom with these young, teenage felons. When I arrived I immediately sensed a different vibe than is common in adult facilities. The tension was palpable, but much more enthusiastic. I walked into the gym and the teens were already seated in two groups on two sections of the bleachers. The average age of this group was 17.8 years old. The prison can hold them as young as age thirteen and keep them as old as twenty-one. These two groups were rival organizations and they were literally sitting right next to one another separated by only a small railing. There were approximately thirty young men in each section making a total of sixty-four in the group overall. Each side had a completely different energy, and it was very apparent who the leaders were.

Typically when I speak to students and in youth detention centers, I try to impress upon them that although they feel as though they are ready to handle state prisons, they are in fact not ready at all. I look around the audience and tell them honestly that I don't see anyone that is built for the places where we typically do our POPP programs: maximum security prisons. However, with this group of Ohio juveniles, that was not the case. As I looked around, it saddened me to see that there were quite a number of these teens that looked quite ready to go to "Big Boy" prison, and I told them so. These were youngsters in grown men's bodies, and they were practicing to graduate to the next level.

One large group of these boys came out of Cleveland and had formed a very dangerous prison gang that developed in the Ohio youth correctional system a little over a decade ago. They recruit heavy and use domination and force to grow their numbers and considerable influence. This gang has now emerged in the adult facilities in the Midwest, as young men graduate to adult facilities in and around Ohio. This organization has been featured on the hit series "Gangland." The other dominant group of teens came out of Cincinnati. They were created as a reaction to their rival gang, and developed as a way to protect the kids coming out of other cities besides Cleveland. The two sides are literally at war with one another in these youth prisons. Now these gangs are growing on the streets as young people get out and continue what they started in prison. This is a real problem and a constant threat to correctional security and the communities that they return to.

So, as I walked to the microphone and prepared myself to address this audience, there was a very heavy tension in the air; you could feel it. The one gang was seated to my right, with their leader lounging back and surrounded by his higher ranking guys. And right next to them were their rivals, with their "number one" laying back and surrounded by his enforcers. I didn't even need to ask who was who, as it was obvious. They gave me their attention, but over the next five hours I had to earn every second of it. I had to work harder, sharper, smarter, and quicker on my feet than ever before. I had four, one-hour sections to fill with nothing but myself and a microphone. That evening they would be given the choice as to whether they wanted to return for the next day—it was a purely voluntary program for seventeen-year-olds in a juvenile prison—and this proved to be quite a challenge. My sole objective for day one was simple: convince them to return for POPP Day Two. Easier said than done.

The next morning I got through security, and made my way back to the gym. As I walked through the prison yard I saw one of the young men from the day before being led through the yard by an officer toward the infirmary. His face was busted up and it was obvious that he had been in a fight. I wasn't sure, but quite possibly he had the signature calling card of the rival gang: a broken jaw. I walked into the gymnasium, and my heart sank. There were only about twenty boys seated at the tables from the group the day before. I quickly began to get my mind right and tell myself that twenty was enough and that at least we had the third that were committed to the POPP program, and that twenty was enough to change a prison. But as I began to meet and greet the young men seated around the room, more teens began filing in behind me. They had been held up during the morning count due to the fight and were subsequently a little late. When everyone was present and accounted for, we had 100 percent participation and every one of those boys had voluntarily come back, much to my surprise. I was filled with renewed energy as I reminded myself what I always teach: "We were built for peace, and everyone is hungry for it, even if they don't know why." Yes, even these young, tough juvenile offenders. You can't find a tougher audience in America, and we hadn't lost even one from the day before; even with the tremendous peer pressure back in their dorms they had each chosen to come back for more.

The objective on Day Two was similar but more focused. I had another six hours with these young men and today I would convince them to sign the peace pledge, wear the wristband, commit to eight weeks of small groups, daily journaling, and a paper writing project. This would prove to be an even tougher assignment than the day before. Some were very excited to be back and they surrounded me to meet, talk, and shake hands. Others were there because they were curious and had seen something on the first day that must have gotten their attention. However, some were there because the rest of their organization was attending, or they were told to be there.

Day Two featured engagement, interaction, questions, and a few simple exercises. I had to persuade them to believe that peace in that institution was not only possible, but that it would greatly benefit them all to work together to achieve it. I had to inspire them, motivate them, challenge them, and even down right dare them to give it a try. A powerful turning point was when I told them that just the night before in the men's facility an hour north in Marion, one of their own gang leaders had graduated the 40 Days to Freedom program and celebrated with the rest of the men in that prison. This was a young man they had all heard of and even possibly interacted with. I was able to recount to them how excited and fired up their brother was at his accomplishment and that he was now committed to be a role model to them of what a peacemaker looks like. That spoke to them, and they were much more interested in how a program could have impacted one of their own. I believe it gave me credibility and respect with this young group of tough kids.

At the end of the day I offered them the 40 Day POPP Challenge. Once again it was up to them; no one was forcing them, and no one would make them engage in this eight week project. In these juvenile facilities they have mandatory classes in the mornings and afternoons, so it's not like they have nothing better to do. This would be a big deal if they voluntarily decided to make room for this in their lives. One of the other challenges to them was where they were deliberately seated in the second half of the second day. They were not allowed to sit in their regular groups with their homeboys. The Cleveland kids were seated with the Cincinnati kids and visa-versa. This did not make them happy, especially the leaders. During the breaks there were small group discussions that broke out, and I am quite sure they were deciding what they were going to do about the challenge. At the end of the day when they were asked to come forward, line up, sign the pledge publicly, put on the POPP wristband, and begin their 40 Day journey together, once again I did not know what to expect. I was so encouraged to see 100 percent of these young men line up and take the 40 Day Challenge, and the staff was amazed. We were about to begin an historic march together, a young march to freedom.

After the second day I was introduced to one of the boys. He was put together, not real big, but strong and athletic. The night before he had been challenged to fight. He responded by telling the other kid: "I'm not gonna fight you tonight. I wanna be in the Power of Peace tomorrow." They didn't fight that night, which was rare for this young man. He was late for Day Two, because the other teen continued to challenge him until he finally gave in. The staff made the decision, which I thought was a good one, to let this boy participate in the program because he had attempted to practice the POPP principles after only one day of training. Although he had chosen to fight, at least he was making an effort to change, and this is the whole point of the project. I walked over and reached out my hand and said, "I'm proud of you, young man. Welcome to the Power of Peace."

CHAPTER 7
AN OUTSIDER
IN A PRISON MOSQUE

I go where I am invited, and now I am in a situation that is fascinating, solemn, and very rare for a white, American follower of Jesus. I am surrounded by black Muslims and joining in on their Juma'ah service, which is the congregational Friday prayer of Islam. This is quite an honor, because non-Muslims must be invited in and can only observe. What is even more remarkable about this occasion is that we happen to be in a maximum security prison, and during a time where there is much tension between the Muslim and the non-Muslims. There has been recent violence between the groups and everyone is on edge, coupled with the fact that this serious outbreak happened during the month of Ramadan. I have become friends with the Imam, and he has extended this honorable invitation. I have butterflies, as I am about to witness something that I have never seen nor experienced.

There are curious looks and occasional stares as I look on respectfully and with a strong, but peaceful tone. Some are not necessarily comfortable with the fact that I am there, while others seem moved by the gesture. The men that I know stop and welcome me with the traditional greeting "As-salamu alaykum" (Peace be unto you) to which I reply "Wa alaykumu as-salaam" (and unto you peace). Whether they agree that I should be there or not, I feel as though I have gained some sort of new street cred for showing the respect to their leader who has invited me. I listen to the prayers, and try to understand the meaning of the Arabic words being so eloquently expressed.

The sermon that is offered makes sense and there is nothing in it that rubs me the wrong way. As we part, some of us hug and we walk out into the prison yard, and I begin to talk to the inmate Imam. He is a beautiful soul named Ronnie. He begins to talk about all the beauty in the world. He speaks as he looks up into the sky: "You can find beauty in anything if you look hard enough for it. Look at that razor wire. Most see bondage, limitations, and struggle. If you look closely you can see the sunlight shimmer off the razor's edge. It's really quite beautiful."

I was amazed. Here was a man who was finding a way to be grateful for the razor wire that kept him bound. But maybe he was freer than many in the free-world, as they call it. I would run into him again several years later, but this time in downtown Atlanta. He walked up to me and flashed his great big smile. At first I didn't recognize him in street clothes, but then I did and we hugged for longer than men typically do. It was a beautiful reunion.

My Personal Walkabout

I decided that after all of those years of doing all the speaking, preaching, teaching, and counseling, that it was time for me to shut up and begin listening. I resolved to become a student of life, science, cosmology, psychology, world faith traditions, neuro-science, quantum physics, and everything else I had never bothered to learn. You see, I had been telling everyone else what to believe for so long that I had not questioned what I really believed for a very long time. So I went on a journey of discovery that has carried on to this day, and I don't plan on ever stopping. I have a thirst for knowledge, and I am fascinated with the way that our Creator has designed this amazing universe.

That one decision has taken me around the world: into ashrams, temples, synagogues, cathedrals, mosques, monasteries, and even a Native American sweat lodge. This sweat lodge initiation was one of the most challenging, grueling, and yet liberating experiences of my life. I was pushed beyond my limits and far beyond what I felt like my body could endure. I was ceremonially prepared by a true elder and medicine man by the name of Blue Wolf after I had fasted for three days to get myself ready for the experience. The sacred stones are heated for hours by fire, and on this day nineteen brothers and sisters gathered into a small earthen lodge carefully and ceremonially constructed from stone, mud, wood, and animal hides. We were packed inside so tight that we were touching one another with no room to stretch our legs, backs, or arms.

There are four rounds and once the lodge is closed we are surrounded with complete darkness. The stones are brought in about four or five at a time. They are so hot that they glow red in the darkness. Between each round there is a short break for water and then four or five more stones are brought in and the heat intensifies. The lodge is closed again, and chants and ceremonial songs are sung and drums are played. By the fourth round the heat has gone up to an almost unbearable 160 degrees. The only way to endure it is to go deep inside and draw from a strength that you do not know you possess. You also have to draw on the strength of the others in that tight circle. We helped each other get through it together, and there was incredible unity among many of us who were previously strangers. I am forever bonded to these beautiful souls as we have gone through a trial by fire together. It was a kind of rite of passage for me into a deeper level of self.

The Native Americans believe that the sacred stones, which are smooth and round from hundreds of thousands of years in the river, carry the spirits and ancient wisdom of their ancestors. They believe that bringing those burning stones into the circle ushers in their ancestors in a very beautiful way for them to impart their wisdom to the people gathered inside the sweat lodge.

As the fourth round ended, we emerged from that tiny lodge into the cool rain back in the woods of North Georgia, and it literally took my breath away. We were taught that we were coming out of the "womb" and experiencing a type of rebirth. It was beautiful, and I was drenched and completely spent. We sat around the medicine circle and shared our experience, and then we all feasted together and celebrated. I will never forget that day. What if I hadn't been open to another way of seeing this world? I would have lost out on some truly life-changing experiences, times that I now treasure and that helped me become a better man.

The POPP Process: Part Two—the Power of the Wristband

Early on in the process, I realized that we needed a constant reminder that we were attempting to do something different and new. The POPP wristband was actually an unintended consequence of our "Hope is the New Dope" T-shirts being discontinued in a prison in Ohio. The warden had allowed us to give the black shirts to the very first graduating class of our 40 Days of Peace program there. These shirts meant the world to them; it was like a badge of honor. The men had done something significant, and they had completed something noble and noteworthy. Nobody had ever asked them to stand up for peace and to be a part of the solution. It turned out that they were ready, willing, and able—all someone had to do was ask. They were not ashamed to wear the POPP shirts through the yard, as a matter of fact they WANTED everyone to know that they were "one of those peacemakers."

However, black clothing is hard to spot at night, and the security officers tend to wear black in most state prisons, so that is why you will not see black uniforms for prisoners and why we received pushback with the POPP shirts. There was also a bit of envy going on and there was considerable demand for this new commodity. So they told us no more "Hope is the New Dope" T-shirts in the prison. They did allow the men who had earned them to keep them, and I see those original POPP jerseys there to this day. My response to this situation was to go to work to figure out something that the states would allow, but that still earned the POPP graduates respect and set them apart behind the razor wire. That is where the idea for the wristband came from.

However, I was still a little concerned that the wristbands might cause the participants to become targets in some of the more dangerous prisons, that other inmates who were jealous would seek them out and cause them harm. I was wrong. The opposite happened: inmates that wore the band began to be treated with a new kind of respect. Other inmates would go out of their way sometimes to give them a pass or stand up for them if need be. Fights would be brewing and someone would come up and say, "Give this brother a break man. Can't you see that he is on his 40 Days of Peace?" I was amazed.

There are now prisons where convicts are actually wearing as many as five POPP wristbands, because they have gone through five phases. We have some prisons where over half the inmate general population are wearing the brand, and violence has dropped dramatically. Many of these men are brilliant and very motivated. All along the way they have helped construct this powerful young peace movement. They have done the heavy lifting. Hope really IS the new dope.

Lights Out at Marion

I was on a prison tour through Michigan and into Ohio where I saw over five hundred inmates graduate different phases of the Power of Peace Project in a single week. I had called one of the wardens at a prison in Ohio where the Prison Peace Initiative had been developed in the early days of the project. There are inmates in that facility who are still wearing those original black POPP T-shirts that the warden allowed them to receive at our very first 41st Day Celebration several years ago. Those early members of the prison peace movement wear those shirts so proudly, and it was a very significant part of the development process. It was very hard for any of those men who were wearing those POPP shirts to be involved in any trouble—they were held to a higher standard and it worked. It was a healthy kind of peer pressure.

So I asked if I could swing through there on my trip and encourage the Power of Peace graduates. The warden agreed and I arrived on a

Thursday evening during that tour. It is always like a homecoming when I go back to these prisons across the country, as I get to see old friends and the men behind the razor wire who have changed my life. As they file into the room, there are hugs, laughter, and lots of catching up. I get to encourage them for the way that their work is effecting the lives of countless people, and how their labor is not in vain.

We began that evening talking about three topics: 1) I have a dream—they share three specific dreams that they have for their lives; 2) I am happiest when—they share three things that make them come alive and feel joy when they engage in them; 3) My best day—they come up with the happiest and best day of their lives, and share it with great detail. It is a powerful exercise. As we shared, suddenly the lights went out and the chapel was completely dark, as there are no windows in the building and all the power in the prison had been shut down. The lights remained out for about fifteen to twenty minutes with around 100 convicts in the room together in close proximity. I joked about how I must really trust them, and they heckled and jeered me lightheartedly. The program went on and we didn't skip a beat. It didn't cross my mind until later that most people would have felt vulnerable, anxious, or afraid in a moment such as this. However, I felt like I was in the safest place in the world. It hadn't occurred to me to be afraid, because I was with my friends. Someone else brought to my attention how much the administration must trust POPP, because they didn't come and shut down the program when the power was cut; they just let us continue. The Power of Peace: large numbers of hated, feared, and forgotten men laughing and fellowshipping in the darkness. Actually there was quite a light in that room that night—a light that most people cannot yet see.

CHAPTER 8
THE DANGEROUS ROUNDTABLE

I was trained for fifteen years in the ministry to be an evangelist and a pastor. I knew how to plant a church, grow a church, and lead a church. I learned how to preach, teach, and counsel. I could lead a men's retreat or a small group discussion, using the Bible to dismantle arguments, untangle conflicts, or heal broken relationships. Years later, there I was in a different type of small group. Surrounded by rival gang leaders and high ranking members in a dangerous prison, all eyes were on me. This was above my pay grade. We were discussing how the peace initiative was coming along and I was fielding questions, comments, and concerns. A hand went up in the back and I called on the gentleman and gave him the floor. "I have a question. This week in our unit a man was tied up, wrapped in a sheet, and set on fire. What should we do about that?" I paused, gathered my thoughts, and opened it for discussion. Then these men of influence debated on how to handle retaliatory violence as a group in the coming weeks. They all agreed to tell their men to stand down with no retaliation, and that we would discuss specific incidents as a group moving forward. Things were changing and I was trying to keep up.

The men at this round table were strong, influential men with a lot of worldly power. The fact that the administration was allowing us to meet together in this small chapel with no officers present was no small thing. There had recently been a large gang fight with multiple stabbings and dozens sent to the infirmary and the hole. The vibe was very intense, especially between two rival groups who were present in the room. The fact that these men were treating one another with dignity and respect was a miracle, and I had a front row seat. We talked of another place and time; we imagined together what the early gatherings in the civil rights movement must have been like. I talked about Martin and the fact that you couldn't march with him if you were unwilling to adopt and operate under the principles of non-violence; not only as a philosophy but as a lifestyle. I asked the group what kind of man would allow himself to be spit on and not retaliate in hatred and anger; to wipe his face and continue to love. A well-known leader named Julio spoke up and said in disbelief, "That man would have to be a beast." And he said that with ultimate respect. Then he continued, "But there's no way Dr. King would have let me march with him!" The men all laughed, but at least they saw that it was possible and had happened before, even in their own lifetimes. Using peacemakers from the twentieth century has proven quite effective. We use the universal and timeless non-violence principles of scripture and all the world faith traditions, and we show that men and women around the world in the last 100 years have used these powerful tools to change their world, and that it could happen again—even with them. "Why not us, and why not now?" Now men in prisons around the country speak not only of those movements but of their POPP principles as well.

These powerful men began to use their influence for peace and things began to change. Violence went down dramatically, and a period of thirty days went by with no stabbings at all—something that hadn't happened for as long as anyone could remember. In the heat of the summer when violence spikes, the officer's walkie-talkies were quiet, as there were very few critical incidents. Gang hits were being reconsidered and sometimes even overturned and called off. A potential riot was averted because the peace council had stepped in and negotiated peace between the two warring parties over an issue of three thousand dollars in cash, which had switched hands and not been returned to the rightful party. Neither I nor the administration ever even knew that happened. The council members were policing their own. The round table was having a considerable impact and the warden and his staff began to take notice.

The Tipping Point

I believe that in the life and evolution of a business, organization, team, or movement, if it achieves extraordinary success, there is a tipping point. What begins as an idea, leads to an experiment, which develops into a practice, then a program, becomes organized, structured and replicated. Somewhere along the growth cycle an interesting point is reached. Whereas all your energy has been spent pushing, and selling, and driving in the beginning, all of the sudden you become aware of a shift in momentum and the universe begins to pull you along, attracting like-minded individuals, collaborators, and partners. It is the overnight sensation or the new artist of the year, who isn't new at all. It's the idea that goes viral and orders go through the roof. It's the sports franchise that has been in a rebuilding mode for several years and then goes on a winning streak, and everyone wants to join that team. In a movement, that tipping point can come by way of many different forms. In the civil rights movement it happened in some dark and heinous acts which finally aroused the conscience of a nation that had been asleep. It had to get the darkest right before the dawn. Marchers being beaten down by the Klan on Bloody Sunday; four little girls being blown up in a church in Birmingham; people of color being attacked with water hoses and police dogs on the nightly news. The tipping point had arrived and the momentum had shifted.

In the Power of Peace Movement there have been a number of significant moments when I felt the momentum shifting. There have been turning points along the way where I sensed that things had changed and they would never be the same again. The first big shift happened when peace was shattered by the killing of an inmate named "Bug." He was stabbed over twenty times by a group of inmates outside the chow hall. After that, a wave of violence swept through that prison so fast that within six weeks there were four dead bodies and a fifth died under mysterious circumstances just a month later; all the result of a gang war that led to a series of retaliation killings. It got so bad that the administration had no choice but to lock the prison down, with no movement, for over a year. No visitation, no education or classes, no faith-based services, and meals brought to their cells. They shipped hundreds of inmates to other prisons and brought in hundreds more. It got national attention and what had once been a dirty little secret was now exposed to the light. There was a huge problem in the correctional system and it wasn't going to get better on its own or go away quietly. I felt for the warden who ended up getting sent to another prison. He is a good man who did a phenomenal job in the toughest of situations. He is a man of faith: honorable, noble, honest, hardworking, and strong. To this day we remain friends, and I am saddened that he bore the brunt of responsibility for a situation that spun out of control.

At the time I thought all of it was a curse. I couldn't understand why it had happened when things were going so well. Things had become so peaceful there for a time, and now it had not only gone back to the way things were, but tumbled into a place that was much, much worse. I asked God why He was allowing it. I looked for answers but could find none. Perhaps the world needed to see the problem that had been locked away and out of sight for so long. However, at least in my world, this changed everything. If Hays would have never gotten shut down, then I never would have considered going outside of my home state of Georgia.

Soon after those events I was invited to go on tour with a wonderful organization called Prison Fellowship through Illinois and Florida state prisons. It was an amazing time: it was me, my friend Gary, and a hip-hop group out of Detroit called the Gideon Crew & Sunny Day. We did two-hour shows, three prisons a day, for four and five days in a row. It was relentless and we were exhausted but elated. I was soon speaking to hundreds of convicts at a time, and I was being invited to speak in more prisons around the country. Seeds were being planted that would bear fruit in the years to come. The Power of Peace Project began to develop and take root in Ohio, and then we grew even more in Michigan, and then next came Kansas and Nebraska. None of this would have ever happened if things hadn't changed so dramatically in Georgia. I believe that God and His universe will use whatever you give Him. He uses the darkest times, sometimes, to bring about the greatest good, and I think that is happening in the world right now. Things are getting very dark, because the sun is about to rise again. Hays is coming back and things are improving. The men still there from the original POPP movement continue to strive for peace. Some have gotten shipped to other prisons and carried on their good work. Peace is still on the move.

CHAPTER 9
MIRACLES IN THE LAND OF MANDELA

I'm stepping off the plane in Johannesburg, South Africa, half way around the world. I'm looking for a small, young Indian man named Raj. We've never met, nor even talked, but he is my connection and I have no plan B. He knows what I look like, but that's about it. Luckily, Raj finds the tall, lanky American and we set off on our adventure. I am finally in the land of Mandela again. I have been intrigued and fascinated with this great man ever since I read "Long Walk to Freedom" years ago. I have always wanted to come back to this historic place and finally it has arrived; the last time I was here was in 1995 after Mandela had been elected president. I have come all this way to try to get a place at the Gandhi Global Peace Summit that will begin in two days in Durban. All I know is that I received a mass email about this conference that is held once every six years. It is hosted by Ela Gandhi, granddaughter of Mahatma Gandhi, and noted civil rights leader Dr. Bernard Lafayette. Freedom fighters and peace icons from around the world meet and discuss solutions for world peace. The fourteenth Dalai Lama is represented, as well as dignitaries from India, Uganda, Egypt, and other war-torn countries from around the world. I just want to be present and sit at the feet of these great people and learn what I have been sent there to learn. I just hope that they will let me in, and that I can get a seat and see the stage from where I am. But I have no idea what is in store for me.

When I learned that I would be making this historic trip, I proclaimed to the church that I would not only be visiting Robben Island where Mandela was incarcerated for eighteen of his twenty-seven years, but that

I would also be speaking in a South African prison. The only problem? I had no connections, invitations, nor did I even know of any specific South African prisons. I just reasoned that I would figure it out when I got there; I do a lot of things like that, and have found that it is a fascinating way to live: call your shot, and then go and search for an open door. My driver and interpreter was a wonderful young Zulu man named Mulu. Halfway into my trip and after the conference had already begun, Mulu called and said that he had a couple of friends who wanted to meet me. I told him that I would be honored and that we could have dinner together that evening. He said that they couldn't meet until late and that there was one more thing that I should know about them: they were former gangsters and had done time inside a place called Westville Prison. That sounded like it would be right up my alley, so I quickly agreed.

We went to a mall in the middle of nowhere at about ten that night. It was an adventure to get there as we drove through red lights so that we didn't have to stop, as Mulu informed me that we would risk being carjacked if we slowed down. We met up with his friends, and we immediately hit it off. They told me about growing up in South African Apartheid, and what it was like to do hard time there. They spoke of the Westville prison that was built to hold seven thousand men, but currently houses twelve thousand. They shared about their change and their conversion behind the walls. I was fascinated. The mall was closing and we had to leave, but as we hugged and made our way to the door, I asked them an important question: "Any way you guys could get me into that prison?" They looked at me a little strange and said that they knew the chaplain. I asked them to see if they could get me in, but then I threw in one more request: "It has to be tomorrow morning." The problem was that it was already eleven at night, and if I was going to get in, it needed to be early the next morning, so that I could make it back for the second half of the conference.

The next morning, Mulu called me early. He said that his friends had phoned him and said that they didn't know if they could get me in but it was worth a try, and to get me there by eight. As we drove into the main complex, I was overwhelmed at the size of this prison. As we approached the gate, I prayed that God would open the door. Thirty minutes later we were inside and getting cleared through security. They took me up a long spiral walkway and put me in a large room with no windows. This part of the prison is old, dark, and dank. We waited for what seemed like a long time and then finally men dressed in orange jump suits began to file in. These were Zulu convicts and many of them had blank stares and deep scars. Many were political prisoners, and others were hardened criminals, while others were just desperately poor people in a bad place. I was told that because of overcrowding, they had a system where they had to share cots with other inmates and when their sleeping time was up other inmates would just kick the bed to let the other man know it was their turn.

Within forty-five minutes, we were dancing and singing, laughing and cheering. Here I was halfway around the world and I was experiencing the same reactions and responses as I did from prisoners in America. The only difference was language and culture, but the hearts were the same. Their living conditions were much more desperate, and their spirits longed even more to be free. Once again I was reminded powerfully that we are all humans and we are all in this thing together. I could see the longing for liberation in their eyes and I could sense it in their spirits. I was amazed how God had led me to the exact men that could get me into the exact prison that I had proclaimed that I would enter just weeks before. Fascinating. As we finished and walked back through the gate, I marveled at what had just happened. I looked at the clock and told Mulu that we needed to get back across town as fast as possible, and that maybe I could still make it to the conference by lunchtime.

As we got back to the university and I ran back to the building where the Peace Summit was being held, I busted through the doors right as lunch was almost over. I hurried to the buffet line and got a plate of the Indian Cuisine and made my way to an empty table to wolf down my food. On my way in through the doors, I ran into a new friend who is the founder of War Resisters International out of New York City, a fascinating and brilliant man with a bald head, thick glasses, and a long white beard. He asked me, "Did you get into the prison, and did you get to speak?" I said with a smile that yes indeed, I had! Then he made his way back into the crowd. As I sat there eating alone, I was interrupted by a nice, polite Indian woman. She was there representing the Premier, and she was involved in the development and implementation of the agenda for this important conference. This meeting is held only once every six years and the speakers are carefully chosen and invited far in advance of this event.

She said, "Excuse me, Mr. Cummings, I have a question for you. We have heard that you visited a prison here in Durban this morning, and that you spoke to the prisoners about non-violence. We would like to know if you would be willing to speak."

I was stunned. Trying to swallow my food in order to be respectful, I replied, "Of course, I would be honored. When would you like for me to speak?"

She quickly said, "Right now." And led me by the arm away from my table and up to the podium.

They began to introduce me immediately and said that I had some things of importance that they would like for me to share. Before I even had time to prepare my remarks, I was holding the microphone. There I was in a T-shirt and blue jeans with Ela Gandhi and Dr. Bernard Lafayette in the front row. But I was honored and privileged to have the very important opportunity to present to peacemakers from around the world about the Power of Peace Movement, and how we were teaching Gandhi, King, and Mandela nonviolent principles in prisons and inner city schools back in the states. I was overwhelmed with gratitude and amazed at what had just happened. It was beyond my wildest dreams, but exactly why I had come all the way across the world. I just didn't know it.

Afterward as we were dismissed to go to our breakout groups, I had the opportunity to interview Ms. Gandhi and Dr. Lafayette. I was standing in front of two civil rights heroes and pioneers, face to face, in the city where Mr. Gandhi started this nonviolent movement over a century before. Both of these icons had a similar message for me as I interviewed them with my flip cam: "Do not stop what you are doing. You are fulfilling Mr. Gandhi's and Dr. King's dream of spreading the principles of non-violence around the world. Martin's final wish was to institutionalize nonviolence. Taking it into the prisons is on the cutting edge of this movement and we are pleased with what you are doing." I was humbled, honored, and overjoyed to be a part of this historic effort.

I had journeyed through the land of Mandela after studying about his life and teaching his nonviolent principles for years. The only thing that hadn't happened as I had planned was meeting with Mr. Mandela personally. It turned out that he was too sick to take appointments, though I had two connections who had told me that they could get me in front of him. However, I was able to film a private message to Mr. Mandela and I thanked him for what he was doing for inmates and kids in America. I was told that he watched it before he died.

Universal Laws and Principles

All that I teach I have borrowed or stolen; only the mistakes are mine. There is nothing new under the sun and truth has always been out there for anyone who wants to seek it, discover it, grab it, and give it away. So I picked these principles up along the way and began to implement them, and I am getting the same results that peacemakers all across history have gotten when they are utilized. They are timeless, universal, and eternal. They work wherever they are practiced, by whomever they are used, in whatever situation they find themselves. The truth is the truth: it does not need to defend itself, prove itself, protect itself, or sustain itself— it just *is*. Truth stands alone and stands the test of time. These principles worked in the racist, bloody, and segregated South when Dr. Martin Luther King picked them up and used them. They worked in Gandhi's colonized India almost a half-century before. They worked in apartheid South Africa when Mr. Mandela used them to put back together a nation on the brink of civil war. And they will work today in any and every conflict on the global stage. Whether it be racial, ethnic, cultural, gender, socio-economic, or religious differences and conflict, these are the solutions. The problem? Getting human beings to submit to the process in humility. That is why it is so extraordinary what these convicts have accomplished. Many of them have submitted their wills and egos, in front of their enemies, in order to establish peace. They are proving that if it can happen there, it can happen anywhere.

They just need a holy mission. The Kings and Gandhis and Mandelas of this world have inspired the masses by their selfless example of courage and nonviolence. But who did they inspire? The common man; the low classes and the suffering; the poor and disenfranchised; the hungry, angry, lonely, and tired ones. They empowered the ones who were being forgotten and left behind, and that is exactly who are rising up now. Jesus said he would be with the hungry, the thirsty, the naked, the stranger, the sick, and the prisoner. Inmates, prisoners, and convicts comprise all six classes. It is an untapped army of peacemakers if we can reach them. Two and half million souls locked up in the land of the free. Just imagine if a peace movement emerged and exploded in that dark place. Wouldn't that be just the way that He would do it? He always does things upside down, and I am just crazy enough to believe that I am witnessing that as we speak: a prison revival. I wish you could see it, because you wouldn't believe your eyes.

CHAPTER 10
THE MIGHTY MEN OF MUSKEGON

We have just finished our 41st Day Celebration at a Michigan maximum security prison. I am elated, as I have just witnessed a miracle. I have seen violent men come together for forty days, putting their beefs aside and sitting down at the table with one another. I have seen convicts cheer for one another as they received their POPP certificates of achievement. I have seen tough men shed tears at the open mic sharing. I have seen high fives and hugs between rival gang members, and even seen a white gang leader read his paper on Dr. King, and share about how it has changed him. These 40 Day Projects have a power and intensity that is hard to describe. These men embrace the principles, own their convictions, and take responsibility for bringing peace to their dangerous community. But the most powerful moment came after the celebration had ended. As the men were walking out, a well-known convict approached me. This man had stood out from the beginning. An enforcer for his organization, he looked the part. Big and strong, he was weathered by many years of incarceration, and he had the scars to prove it. He had been seated right next to his boss during the 40 Day Project, for his protection, and his leader was chosen to share at the open mic night. Larger than me, the enforcer looked me in the eye and said he needed to talk to me.

He began, "This project has saved a life." I told him that I agreed and that it had probably saved a number of lives across the country. He said, "No, I mean that it saved a life here on this yard." He went on: "An order had been given, and the decision made that a guy had to go. I was the one that was sent, because that is what I do. I walked all the way across the yard to go and see him. I got to his building, and I looked down and saw this damn wristband. I couldn't dishonor the movement; I couldn't disrespect the band. So I turned around and walked all the way back across the yard. I had decided that I would return to my cell and remove the wristband, and then I would go back and do him. But that walk gave me time to think and reconsider." He stopped and his eyes filled with tears and his lip began to quiver. "I'm telling you that a man on this compound is still breathing because of this peace pledge, and I just wanted to thank you." He quietly turned and walked away, as I stood there speechless. Once yet again, I felt as if I was standing on holy ground.

I had initially been invited to this prison because of gang violence and retaliations that were causing serious security threats. This was perfect timing as I needed a facility similar to Hays in order to test the principles and further develop the POPP program. If I could have chosen a place to test the Hays Experiment, it would not have been Muskegon, Michigan. I had never even heard of Muskegon, nor did I know where it was. It happened to be perfect though. In the western part of the state, not far from Lake Michigan, is a small town that happens to have three prisons in very close proximity to one another. One is maximum, one is medium, and one is minimum security. Together they house approximately five thousand male offenders. I was invited there by an amazing warden who has become an advocate and mentor to me. I call her "Miss Mary." I met her at a conference where we were both speaking, and she shared with me about recent gang violence that they were experiencing at the high security facility in Muskegon. I accepted her invitation, and an amazing journey began for the Power of Peace Project. I needed an institution where I could have the time, the access, and the freedom to test the principles that we had effectively utilized at Hays, and to see if they could be replicated. Miss Mary provided exactly that. Over the next two years we would see well over 1500 convicts in those three prisons engage in the peace effort. Though it is difficult to obtain hard numbers in such a short amount of time, off the record, Warden Mary has stated that violence dropped by as much as fifty percent there and that critical incidents were three to five times lower than other high security facilities in the state; and much credit was given to the Power of Peace program. The curriculum was being further developed and the project began to have structure and a more well-defined process. The Hays Experiment was becoming what I began to call the "Muskegon Model."

Leadership behind the Scenes

The key to the shift that happened there was getting the leaders to buy into the program and begin to own it. Some of the most powerful men in the prison already had great respect and love for Warden Mary, and this was why they were willing to try it in the first place. However, as they began to see the results, they began to believe that this could be something that could actually change their environment and lead to a better quality of life for those that had to live there. They embraced the principles and things began to change rapidly. One man stands out at the maximum security facility, much the same way that Dre did in our first. The first few times I spoke at this particular prison, he stood out to me. He sat near the back all by himself, his arms were crossed, and he wore a scull-cap. He happened to be on the smaller side, but I got the feeling that the others kept their distance out of respect. No one sat near him on the row that he chose, and he remained very still, with his legs crossed. There was no expression on his face, and when the others laughed or clapped, he remained quiet. When the meeting was over I noticed that he seemed to be "holding court" at the back of the gym as other inmates gathered around him or came to speak to him individually. He appeared to be a man of influence in this place. He was one of the most influential leaders of the Moors, a sect of Islam, in that high security prison, and they called him "Lynch-Bey."

There was another man there that also got my attention that very first day, and we have been friends ever since. He was a big man, physically strong, with piercing eyes that stared right through you. He happened to be one of the most powerful Christian leaders at the facility. Every time I saw him he gave me a big bear hug, and said in a deep voice, "How are you doing, Saint?" And he was not asking out of habit. He stared deep into your eyes and said, "No, how are you really doing, brother?" They call him "Potts."

I have grown very close to both of these men and it is inspiring to watch them work together for a common purpose. They have been doing that on some level for some time now inside this Michigan state prison. Both have been there a very long time, and both have a large following who pay close attention to what they say and especially what they do, and how they carry themselves. This young peace movement would not take hold or last without the buy-in of these two brothers from very different worlds. These two men became very important to the communication process. They had meetings with the warden on a regular basis and with myself when I return every couple of months. This was crucial as we were trying to build a prison peace movement in Michigan, while I lived hundreds of miles away in Atlanta.

On one of my visits to Muskegon at this particular facility, I discovered that we had a problem. As I walked across the prison yard escorted by an officer, a prisoner yelled in my direction, "Hey Kit, you got a minute?" I walked over his way and recognized him as we got closer. He approached me and I reached out to shake his hand and give him the "convict hug." He was unusually distant, which was a surprise. He had become a friend and a part of the movement, and I hadn't seen him for a few months. "How come I wasn't allowed into the new forty day program? I graduated the first two and they are telling me that I can't be in the next one." He wasn't happy with me, and he turned his back on me and walked away. I was a little confused and definitely surprised by it. This program has become so popular that the demand has increased each time, and now over half the prison population have expressed interest. This was causing a problem, as there was too much demand and not enough space, staff or facilitators to handle it. So this brother had been left out of the mix and he was not happy about it. The more I asked around, the more I discovered that it wasn't just one guy. The rumor mill was buzzing and guys were talking. This is a very tight knit community and messages spread quickly, whether true or not. There was a vibe among the veterans of the Power of Peace movement at this institution and it was not positive.

These men have learned not to trust, not to hope, and to prepare to be hurt. They have learned that people lie to you, never show up, always eventually leave, and will eventually let you down. They do not let themselves get close to one another, not really, because eventually their hopes will be crushed again. So they play it safe, stay on the defense, and harden their hearts. But something powerful happens when they go through these forty day projects. They begin to hope again, open their hearts, make new friends, and even begin the trust process. They begin to expect new results and they begin the long road to healing. They get hooked on peace and they develop a hunger for more, and when someone tries to take it away from them they fight for it, which is good.

However, it is very easy to go back to what they know; back to what has been proven to them over and over again. So the word spread that I was upset with them, and that I was disappointed in their effort. They believed that I was punishing them by refusing to let them into the next phase and even that I was not coming back. None of that was true, but that was the story. There was a communication problem and silence typically communicates a negative. Left unsaid, messages can be misinterpreted and we begin to create stories for what we feel must be true— we all do it to some degree. They wrote me an open letter from some of the group expressing their concerns, their disappointment, and their discouragement. They believed that I wasn't practicing the POPP principles and that I wasn't upholding the honor and integrity of the movement. On one hand I was disheartened by the letter, but on the other hand I was impressed by the way in which they were coming together and taking a stand—fighting for their peace project.

I did the only thing that I could think that would work to bring about a resolution. I asked the warden if she would set up a private meeting with myself, Mr. Linch-Bey and Mr. Potts. She agreed, they were called out, and we met in a room all alone. I asked them if what I was hearing was true and they confirmed that indeed it was. They went overboard assuring me that the leaders did not feel those things or believe what was being said, but that there was a morale problem that had to be interrupted and redirected in order to maintain the momentum of the movement and keep the violence down. We put our heads together and figured out the root, the cause, the reason for the escalation and the solution to the problem. We went to the warden and asked respectfully if we could create a new phase for these men who had been left out and if they could be personally invited to re-engage. She gave her blessing and we further fleshed out the new plan. But there was one more very important part of the resolution: Potts and Linch-Bay would need to gather the leaders, vouch for me, and spread the word that I was genuine, sincere, and more committed than ever to the struggle and that they could still trust me.

I count both of those men brothers and friends. A black Christian, a white Peace activist, and a black Muslim working together to bring about peace in a very dangerous environment. With all that is going on in the world with conflict, violence and tension between Christian, Muslims, and Jews; blacks, whites and Latinos; nations and religions tearing each other apart, here were brothers working together in the least likely place, and doing something together that possibly the world would never see. But I saw it, and I'll never forget it.

Just recently I saw another one of the Mighty Men of Muskegon step up and exert his considerable influence for peace. We had a POPP graduation for a whole new group of new peacemakers and I asked some of the former grads to share. A man they called Harden-Bey got up and began to share about his journey with the Power of Peace. He has been incarcerated for thirty-seven years and didn't know when or if he would go home. For a man like Harden-Bey, with the influence that he has in this prison, to choose to become a leader for peace and risk his reputation was really quite remarkable. He stood and said the following words to both his peers and enemies alike: "I have been locked down for almost four decades. Many times I've put a knife into a man because I thought I had to. I can tell you today that time and time again, I did it because I was afraid. I was a violent man because I was a punk. Today I can admit that, but until I was able to admit to myself that I was a coward, I could never become a real man. It takes true courage to be a peacemaker, and today that is what I am." Then he went on to challenge them to follow his lead and make peace with one another. He was still leading, but now with another more noble cause: a true man of peace.

The POPP Process: Part Three—the Lost Art of Journaling

Changes like these men are experiencing don't just happen because you accept a challenge or sign a pledge. They come about through true soul searching and digging deep to find out who you really are. That is particularly tough in a prison environment because you rarely if ever get time truly to yourself. This is why the POPP journal is so important. In today's ever changing world of technology, one of the things that is being sacrificed and left behind is the art of writing. This young generation is growing up on hand held devices and smart phones, and within our lifetime we will no longer see the need for paper; and that will be a good thing for the sustainability of our planetary resources and global health. However, we are raising up a generation that has never learned how to express themselves the way that their parents and grandparents before them communicated. Poetry, verse, and sonnets are being replaced by text messages and tweets. Technology, like anything, has positive and negative consequences. Young people are losing the ability to connect with the spoken word, and journaling as a way to get in touch with deep things within is a foreign notion.

However, in prisons the journal is very valuable. These men cherish these little books because they are a gift from the free world and have wisdom within. They take these POPP journals back to their cells and use them. They carry a pen on them wherever they go, and the journals are made pocket-size for a reason. Some men who do not even know how to read and write allow others to help them along and the journal becomes a tool to bring about unity. The men who truly put their hearts into the project get the most out of it. You should see what these convicts produce: brilliant ideas, epiphanies, solutions, and breakthroughs. Some of the papers I have read have been the best works on these peacemakers that I have ever encountered, and I've been studying these icons for quite some time.

As they complete the action challenges for the day after meditating on the Freedom Fighter Quotes that morning, they carry the journal and write down things they see, hear, feel or say. At the end of the day they write down failures or what they learned along the way. It helps some of these men to get in touch with their pain, inner conflicts, and lost convictions. It has become one of the most powerful parts of the peace project. These daily journaling exercises help prepare them to write letters to the next generation; young minds who are preparing to come and see them one day. So they write and express how they feel, what their dreams are, and the lessons they have learned. I have literally thousands of papers, letters, and works that convicts have provided POPP along the way, because it has become a wonderful part of the project. When I leave the institution after another successful forty day journey, the wardens deliver yet another folder of hundreds of letters that allow us to look into the hearts and minds of these feared, hated and forgotten men. These letters are being utilized to help remove the shame and stigma for the families of the incarcerated, as well as to inspire the next generation to break the cycle and find a better way. These men continue to make a difference.

CHAPTER 11

CONVICT POKER AT ANGOLA

Motivation is a powerful force. It is amazing the lengths to which a person will go, and the depths a person can be pushed to when properly motivated. I am witnessing this first hand as I am in attendance at the world famous Angola Prison Rodeo. Angola State Prison is the biggest prison in the US, housing over six thousand inmates with the majority serving life without parole. Once known as the bloodiest prison in the world, Angola has gone through a radical restoration over the past twenty years. This is the fiftieth anniversary of the convict rodeo and thousands are in attendance seated in an outdoor stadium constructed for this event. I have grown close to a number of men who reside in this prison built on eighteen thousand acres of rural Louisiana farmland. Once a slave plantation, it is bordered on three sides by the Mississippi river. I have a friend in Angola Prison who has been there for over fifty years. He has been at Angola longer than I have been alive. Tall, strong, and tough, you would never know that Mr. Starks is eighty-two years old. It is as if prison has preserved him. He has been an elder in the prison church for over thirty years, and he has taught me things about life at Angola that are invaluable. Why would I not listen to a man with his wisdom, experience, and life lessons? He has shared stories with me about that place that have helped me understand my work better, as well as the human condition.

This is a real rodeo with inmates who look forward to this all year long. Black, white, and Latino prisoners leave everything inside the rodeo ring as the crowd cheers and roots them on. Before and after the event, inmates sentenced to life (and in Louisiana life means natural life, with no parole) set up booths and get to sell their wares to free world guests there on the prison grounds. Several items that have been made for me there by the men in blue have become some of my most valued possessions: an alligator wallet made from a gator they pulled out of the Mississippi, an ink pen my brother Larry made from a deer antler, and a belt made from a rattlesnake my friend Griffin killed on the prison grounds. This is a working farm that produces corn, soy, beef, cat fish and many more products that are sold in the free world on the open market for quite a profit, and this famous prison operates in the black financially which is almost unheard of. The warden is a world renowned prison reformist that brought God into this prison and changed everything.

The events that are held at this particular rodeo are not your normal rodeo events. They do have some calf roping, barrel racing, and bull riding, but it is their unique prison rodeo events that set this place apart. Early in the competition the crowd watches a round of "Convict Poker." Four inmates are seated at a red card table in the middle of the rodeo ring, and they are playing poker (supposedly). A huge bull with real horns longer than my arm waits in a stall, and he is agitated. When he is released into the arena, the first thing he sees is that red table, and it appears as if he cannot believe four men are sitting in the middle of his ring. He snorts and kicks his hoof into the dirt, as he puts his head down and gathers a full head of steam before he reaches his target. Now, the game is this: the last convict to remain seated at the card table wins five hundred dollars in cash money on their books. That might not seem like much in the free world, but in this place it will make you a rich man and definitely change your lifestyle. You would not believe how high a human being can fly when helped along by a two thousand pound bull! Three men lay crumpled in a pile on the dismantled table, and the rodeo clown helps them to their feet as they grin and the crowd cheers wildly. Another struts across the ring triumphantly and raises his hat in the air.

The very last event, and the one that everyone came to see, is a true spectacle; all the convicts, probably fifty in number, are gathered in the arena. The biggest, baddest bull awaits them. He is being poked and prodded and severely disturbed in his stall and cannot wait to be freed. He has a red medallion tied to his forehead. The game is this: whichever inmate can successfully remove and retain that medallion gets five hundred dollars. This becomes a free-for-all as convicts are chasing an angry bull and also strenuously competing with one another to wrestle the chip away from his massive, butting head. It is quite fascinating to watch. The announcer speaks over the loud speaker and says, "Ladies and gentlemen, it is time for what you have all been waiting for. Our reigning champion, Mr. Smith has won this event seventeen times in a row. He is the favorite." Imagine the odds: the same man has managed to beat out dozens of other convicts and get that chip *seventeen* times in a row. He obviously is very motivated, gifted in this area, and has a better strategy than all of the others. The gates open and the bull blasts out of the stall. All you can see is a cloud of dust and convicts bouncing around and flying through the air. Every few seconds the bull emerges from the dust and then the men swallow him up. You guessed it: running out of the crowd and holding the medallion over his head triumphantly is exactly who everyone expects it to be: for the eighteenth time in a row it is Mr. Smith. Unbelievable. Desire, motivation, and a good plan make for a powerful combination.

On one of my trips to this fascinating place, I visited the inmates on death row. The building that houses the prisoners that have been given the death penalty in Louisiana had recently been relocated and constructed on the very back side of Angola. The former building which housed the row sits at the front of the prison grounds and is old, but still functional. I actually spent a whole weekend there, sleeping in one of those tiny cells that had been occupied by convicts that lived there before they eventually met their ends by means of the chair or injection. It was our living quarters during a weekend event called "TURN" that was held at Angola, where we spent twelve hours a day with the residents, most of whom will live out the rest of their natural lives in the middle of rural Louisiana. There was an energy in that cell that I had never experienced before or since.

As we walked from one cell to another in the new death row housing unit, there were very different responses from those we saw through the bars. Some were asleep, while others read their books or stared at their television. Some were happy to see visitors, while others gave us a look that communicated for us to stay away. To the men who looked open, we engaged in light conversation and offered words of encouragement and friendship. These men rarely if ever have visitors any more, and they do not get time with one another—much different from my experience on Alabama's death row. They spend twenty-three hours alone in their eight by ten feet cells, with one hour out for a shower or time outside in a cage. Many say that this is exactly what these men deserve, but I am not going to speak to that issue; I just feel as though I am called to visit with them.

As I walk toward another tiny cell, I see a young man looking away in what seems to be disdain or apathy. He doesn't make eye contact, and several volunteers have attempted, without success, to read scriptures to him aloud. He pays no attention to them. I look in through the bars and I notice a picture of Kim Kardashian on his wall, in all her fit, trim beauty. It is the only piece of art which hangs in this space and obviously it means something to him, in a place where there is nothing beautiful to look at. I look at the picture and then over at him. He catches my eye, and I glance back at the masterpiece hanging on the wall.

"I've got some bad news for you, Bro," I say. He looks at me with a strange look on his face. "She doesn't look like that anymore, man."

He stands up and walks over to the cell door. "What do you mean?" he replies.

"Well, she just doesn't look like that right now, that's all." I say once again.

We begin to converse and I let him in on the fact that she is now very pregnant, and that she has gained about 100 pounds. He looks rather disappointed, but then his eyes brighten and with a small grin he says,

"She's still bad though, ain't she!" I agree and we share a laugh. I reach through the bars and extend my white hand to shake his, which happens to be black, now that we have made a connection. He shakes my hand firmly and then he looks down and notices a tattoo on my forearm. It is actually part of an elaborate tattoo that runs from my wrist all the way up to my shoulder on the inside of my right arm. It is an artwork about peace, with symbols, designs, and words in different languages, and from cultures and faith traditions from around the world. It tells the story of the Power of Peace Movement and chronicles my travels around the globe over the past five years, and it has become a part of our POPP Brand that kids all want to see and get pictures of. The tattoo that gets his attention is the Arabic symbol for Salaam, or peace.

I look down and see the Quran sitting on top of the pile of the many books he has in his cell, and I say respectfully, *"As-salaam alaikum."* To which he replies, *"Wa-alaikum-salaam."* He introduces himself, as do I, and the other volunteers look over at us curiously.

He asks me a very solemn question: "Why are you here?"

To which I reply, "Because I love you."

He quickly questions my response, "How can you love me, you don't even know me?"

I carefully reply, "I might not know you, or how it feels to have to live in this place, but I do know that if I had to be here, then I would want someone to come and visit with me, and to say what I just said."

He looked right through me and said, "Your book says that if you love your brother, then you should be willing to lay down your life for him. Well, if you love me, would you die for me, brother?"

I hesitated and pondered the question, and then slowly responded, "I do not know if I am that kind of man, or if it came down to it, if I would die for you, my brother; but I hope I'm that kind of man."

He smiled and said, "Finally, now that's what I'm talkin' about— honesty." We shook hands again and I walked on, hoping that I would be able to visit with him again someday. I will not forget him, or the question he asked me which is deeply engraved in my mind to this day.

Hope Is the New Dope

A powerful shift in the POPP movement came when I began getting invited to schools in the communities where I was doing the prison work. Invariably someone hears about the peace movement spreading through the prison. An officer might go back and tell a friend, or a chaplain might go back and tell his or her church family, or a volunteer goes out and begins to share about it in the community, or sometimes I will be heard on a radio or TV interview and the word spreads. People love to share good news and the Power of Peace Project is quite a compelling story. Eventually the schools hear about it and invite me to come speak to the kids. The first time I shared the Power of Peace story with a gym full of fourteen to eighteen-year-olds, I did not realize the effect it was going to have on them. Crowds of kids who do not listen to anyone were eerily silent and hung on every word. Rambunctious teenagers and unruly pre-teens were fascinated and gave their full attention for an entire hour. They laughed and cheered and were inspired by what these hated, feared, and forgotten men were doing behind the wire. And the principal and teachers were amazed.

But why were these hard-to-engage young people so interested in POPP? It was because they are already watching: their video games glorify violence; their music romanticizes gangsters and thugs; their social media celebrates the celebrity who gets arrested and goes to rehab. They watch *Hard Time*, *Locked Up*, and *Scared Straight*; they play *Grand Theft Auto* and *Call of Duty*; they have beats that pump profane lyrics and songs about loose women and weed straight into their impressionable minds. They have stopped paying attention to what their brains are paying attention to, and they have begun to unknowingly learn the "convict code" through their entertainment. So when I come in and say, "The Power of Peace Project was born inside Georgia's most dangerous and violent maximum security prison, in the midst of a gang war," that gets their attention, and keeps it.

However, these kids also need modeling from young people in the free world that they can look up to. From the beginning my dream has been to recruit and train college students from local universities to be role models and facilitators for the high school kids and middle school students that we are engaging in the Teen Peace Movement. Now it is becoming a reality: we have begun an internship and volunteer training program with Kennesaw State University in Atlanta. Our first official college intern from that school was Christopher VanDevere. Chris is an outstanding young man with big dreams and a bright future, and he recently graduated with a major in communications. He is planning to move to Brazil soon where he intends to plant seeds for the Power of Peace Project there. He will always be the first full-time intern, but definitely not the last. KSU has over thirty thousand students now, and recently at a POPP presentation for criminal justice and social work majors we had almost 100 percent of the students in the class express interest in serving with the Power of Peace Project for teens. We have become a student organization at KSU and the next step is to hold rallies on campus and promote the peace movement to college kids who are looking for direction. We will develop the college training model there and then take it to other campuses around the country.

Teenagers in our communities are already tuned into the gangster culture in their music, games, movies, and media; they just need role models who speak their language. Through POPP they begin to find unlikely role models in unexpected places. We read them papers that have been written by men inside places that they do not want to go. However, this is not "Scared Straight," but rather "Inspired Straight." These men are changing and trying to fix up what they messed up and striving to be role models to a lost generation that is already following them. These convicts are already role models, it's just a matter of getting them to model a different lifestyle.

What the inmates in our correctional system lack is hope and a noble purpose. Most have just resigned themselves to a life of little or no expectations, pain, loneliness, and suffering. Disconnected from the outside world, they quickly lose hope and begin surviving on base and sometime animal instincts. And then the Power of Peace comes along. They are called to be the solution, and they are given a great big WHY: because the little ones are watching. For many, that is enough. That's all they needed: to be called, challenged and then given the tools that they need. I get to witness them come alive as they have something to get up for early in the morning, stay busy with during the long days, and sometimes keep them up late into the night. New friendships are forged, the environment gets healthier, and they begin to dream that they can become good fathers, brothers, and sons again. And now the young ones are watching too.

CHAPTER 12
THE HEALING IN MEXICO

I am getting "shook down" and inspected very thoroughly as I get through the gate in a Mexican maximum security prison. There are guards high above, up on the walls with AK-47s. This is where high risk inmates deep in the heart of Mexico are incarcerated. I am not sure what to expect as I prepare to speak to about three hundred convicts dressed in khaki uniforms. I am accompanied by my friend and mentor Johnny Moffitt, a former motorcycle gang member from Texas. Having been locked up in the seventies, he loves convicts and they love him. He has been doing this for almost forty years and has been in prisons all over the world. He and I met when we were booked to speak at the same prison ministry conference in Orlando and were mistakenly put in the same room, and literally had to sleep in beds that were four feet from one another. We have been friends ever since.

Speaking with an interpreter is an interesting experience. There is a rhythm that develops and it becomes like a dance. Unlike speaking to American audiences, you have time to think of your next sentence for longer than usual. The inmates look at you, then look at the translator and respond. There is a delay before they laugh or cheer and it is fun to wait for it. These men are intense and hang on every word. In the crowd I know there are cartel members, drug dealers and murderers, but they are not what you would imagine. After the message, they line up to come and pay their respects and ask questions; more so than in US prisons. They are so grateful, at least they are with us. I would not know how they act when we leave or before we come; I just know that around us there is a mutual respect and dignity, regardless of our differences.

Our host is a beautiful evangelical church in Puebla, about an hour from Mexico City. The pastor there is a former Miss Mexico and she and her husband lead a ministry that is exploding with a number of different locations in multiple cities with tens of thousands of converts. Because her churches are not mainstream and are growing so fast, she has been heavily persecuted by the more powerful religious denominations down there as well as those practicing the occult. There have been plots to kidnap her and kill her from time to time, and they live on a compound with high walls and armed guards to protect them. But still she boldly preaches and her churches continue to grow. Her driver is a former government body guard who now works for her to provide protection and security. We preached at her church several times while in Puebla and our team stayed on the compound. These were the most hospitable Christians I have ever met, and I have met them all around the world.

What made this trip a little different and definitely more difficult was the fact that I had broken my shoulder pretty badly just a few days before the trip. The doctor had told me that I shouldn't travel and that I would need surgery to repair the broken shoulder joint. Well, there was no way that I was going to cancel this trip and that was all there was to it. So he set me up with a super-sling that not only kept my arm in the right slot but also wrapped around me and held my arm tight against my body. With a little pharmaceutical help, I was on my way to Mexico. I figured it would only help in some of the dangerous places we were going!

That Friday evening we had a large worship service in this mega-church. I had mentioned to Pastor Sheets, who was leading our team, that I wanted him to have our team pray that I wouldn't need surgery when I got back to the states, because I didn't have time for it. Pastor Sheets has been preaching all over the world for over fifty years and has done this type of service many, many times. He began by saying to the large audience, "The Lord spoke to me this evening, and He told me that we needed to have a healing service. You see we have this young man on our team who recently broke his shoulder. The doctors have told him that it will require surgery, but he doesn't agree with that. Tonight we are going to pray for him." Now you must understand that I wasn't raised in this type of church. These were Holy Ghost Christians and just didn't fit into my box. I was quite uncomfortable that he had called me out. He went on: "I'd like to ask this young man to stand up, right there on the front row." I was embarrassed, and my face turned blood red. I reluctantly stood up and they began to cheer for me. I wanted to sit back down, but then he started to sing in one of the most beautiful voices of prayer that I had ever heard.

I still didn't believe in what he was doing, but I wasn't going to get in the way of this beautiful gesture. Slowly, one by one, beautiful Latino worshippers began making their way to the front and they began to lay their hands on my shoulder. I was resisting gently, until I finally closed my eyes and endured it. Suddenly I heard what seemed to be a very clear voice, but no one was speaking to me. It said, "Are you really going to be so arrogant that you do not accept the gift that I am trying to give you?" I slowly lifted my good arm above my head and just let go. I focused on the song, the vibe, and the spirit of this wonderful, loving congregation and went with it. We finished that night with lots of hugs and a few tears, and then we continued with our prison tour. I can't tell you that my shoulder was immediately healed, for that is not my story. But I can tell you that when I went back to the Emory University Specialist in Atlanta upon my return, he looked at the new x-rays and scans and told me that I did not need surgery any more. Today my right shoulder, the one that I had broken, is much stronger and more mobile than my left shoulder. I had learned a very valuable lesson: stop thinking you know when you don't know, and stop trying to put Him into your own box. He doesn't live in boxes, nor does He fit.

The POPP Steps: 40 Days to Peace

As I began to get outside of the religious box that I had constructed over the years, I began to realize that limitations and boundaries were really just chains that I had bound onto myself. Whatever I believed was possible was my limit, my glass ceiling. So I began to push myself and try new things. That led to the development of the challenge that I began to give hardened criminals in tough prisons. Every man likes a challenge; something that pushes him beyond himself, and that is what the Pledge does.

On January 18, 2011, twelve men signed the first POPP peace pledge in our very first maximum security prison. I had come up with seven non-violent principles that I challenged them to live by for forty days. I reasoned that forty days was long enough to get results and build new habits, but not too long to overwhelm the participant. The steps that I constructed and developed were what I believed to be the keys to stopping violence between prison rivals before it ever even started. All of them are found woven through all the scriptures and faith traditions throughout the ages. These are very simple, but powerful if practiced daily:

1) I will be a peacemaker wherever I go today
2) I will treat all people with respect, even my enemies
3) When provoked I will not retaliate in kind; I will find a better way
4) When cursed I will not curse back; I will pause and use deliberate language
5) I will not lie, cheat or steal
6) When wrong, I will promptly admit it and quickly make amends
7) I will treat all people with the respect with which I wish to be treated

It took several weeks of discussing, debating, and sometimes arguing over these steps before the twelve were ready to attempt them for forty days in a row. Imagine them trying to get their heads wrapped around not retaliating when provoked, or not cursing back when cursed; it goes against everything they have ever learned or been taught in prison culture. We were testing these timeless principles, because I absolutely believed that they would work *anywhere*. Every week we would come back together and review the week before. The twelve would talk about victories and how they had held to their commitment at the gym, in the chow hall, the dorms, or on the yard when confronted with testing or conflict. Sometimes they would share about how they had failed and that it was too heavy or too much for them to bear. Other times we would encourage a brother who didn't believe he could make it, or challenge a young man who was not making a sincere effort. They held one another to a high standard and called one another out when they gave way to weakness or apathy. I learned as I watched them work together and grow.

These principles give participants something to focus themselves, anchor themselves, and guide themselves through challenges and opposition. By following the POPP principles and repeating the steps over and over, a change begins to take place along the way. New patterns, pathways, and habits are developed in the brain and lives begin to change. By coming together with like-minded people on a regular basis, you draw strength from others and borrow their faith when yours is weak. These men are proving that Seven Step recovery is powerful and effective.

CHAPTER 13
CROWD SURFING WITH THE YOUNG BLOODS

Once again I am overflowing with joy as we celebrate the graduation of 40 Days to Peace by another two hundred high risk inmates at a prison in the Midwest. Most of these men come out of the tough streets of Detroit and they are in Level Four, which is the highest security level in this prison, which means that they did something to earn the right to be at that level. We have preached, we have commended, and the men have shared, congratulated, and even hugged their rivals. This is a moment of jubilation as we have the hip-hop group Gideon Crew & Sunny Day performing a concert and we have prepared a feast for these inmates, something that they rarely, if ever, get. As we dance and celebrate I notice a group of young inmates from a particular, well-known organization. They sat together for the first two days of the POPP launch, and in the beginning they were very hard to manage. They made a point of being a bit disruptive during my messages and they would talk to each other and carry on business, which drew intense stares from other convicts in the gym. This can be a problem at events and programs in prison if it continues unchecked. They didn't seem to care, as they represent a new type of convict in the US correctional system: the young, tough, fearless, sometime ruthless, inmate. Many have come up through the youth system, and now they are trying to make a reputation, and the older men don't know what to do with them; and these younger men don't seem to respect the convict code. Back in the day the older convicts would work things out when they had a problem, man to man, one on one, with their hands. Now the rules of the game have changed: now it's often three on one with weapons. That's all the young ones know, but the older guys don't respect that. This makes for a very intense vibe when they are together in one place, because typically the warden doesn't allow these organizations in the same room together at this level of security.

The young men in the back begin to get a little more boisterous than normal. Suddenly they charge toward the stage. The warden, deputy warden of security and the security threat group sergeant are in the back of the gym. They notice the move—and are prepared to handle this situation with security if need be—but all six of them are headed toward me. This is a moment where time stands still. Completely aware and once again trapped in the present moment, there is no time to be afraid; things just happen quickly. I had no idea why they were coming at me, because most of these inmates love me and would never let anyone harm me without some very serious consequences. But they are coming and there is nothing I can do about it. So when they reach me, I brace myself. They grab me, lift me up, and begin to throw me around— it is kind of like crowd surfing.

They were so filled with joy and caught up in the moment that they had decided to toss me around in celebration. It was amazing that anyone even had the idea, much less the inclination to carry it out. All the other convicts laughed and cheered, and even the officers and wardens laughed and allowed them to continue to enjoy themselves. Every time I go back to that maximum security prison, those young guys remind of what they did that day: "Hey Kit, you remember when we threw you around!" Yeah I remember, it's another day I will never forget.

The POPP Process: Part Four—The Magic of the Small Group

Everyone tends to group up somehow in prison—most feel like they have to. So one of the most powerful elements of the forty day project are the weekly small groups. We purposely arrange the seating so that the participants are not sitting with the guys that they normally hang with. The idea is to get all types together in a group, so that they can "walk together" with brothers that they do not know for six weeks. It is quite an interesting vibe in the first week, as Christian, Muslim and Jew; black, white and Latino; old and young; west side and east side; Crips, Bloods, Folks, Gangster Disciples, Vice Lords, Latin Kings, and Arian Brotherhood sit down at the table together. Many times these guys aren't even allowed in the same room, much less the same table. Wardens were willing to take a chance and we experimented: would these men respect the new code and act peacefully for the hour and a half that we would meet together each week? Would they really practice the principles, or would violence erupt? Would they interrupt, ignore, disrupt, or talk over one another? The answer was that they treated one another with unbelievable respect in those meetings and the same thing has happened across the country where it has been tried. There is an unwritten code among these men: honor among thieves. When someone is trying to live peacefully, most times he is given a pass. Not everyone will join the movement, but everybody seems to respect it.

Typically the warden, deputy warden, or chaplain helps us choose eighty-four men—seven tables of twelve works really well—with a good racial, religious, and age balance. Opinion leaders are invited, both positive and negative. I do not want just model inmates and faith-based regulars, and I do not want just gang leaders and troublemakers. I want a good balance of leaders and men of influence. If we can turn the leader into a peacemaker, then we can quickly turn the tide of a facility and reach the tipping point more quickly. After the first day of training and half way through the second day, the men are assigned seats at their "family tables." We arrange seven tables of twelve men each. Each of the seven tables is given a Champion of Peace for their table identity: there is the King table, the Gandhi table, the Mandela table, the Mother Teresa table, etc. They come together once a week at an assigned time and place and they begin the ninety minute program. They sit at the same table every week, and with the same group. They begin by watching a fifteen minute Power of Peace DVD that highlights the POPP Step for that week. It also reinforces the Attitude Science principle for that step that we have already gone through during the program launch. After the video they take out their journals and turn to the corresponding week, and review their progress. At the end of each of the six parts in the journal there are discussion questions that prompt lively and deep conversations among the group. Guidelines are established and the men are reminded each week of the ground rules: one man talks at a time; every man gets a chance to share if he wishes; no interrupting; no excessive cursing; no references to individual "organizations"; no cross-talk; each man is to share only about his own journey and not criticize another man's walk; and no complaining, excuse making or blaming.

The groups develop their own identity along the way. They learn to work as a team and an amazing change takes place. When they sit across the table from one another each week and listen to their rivals, it is much harder to hate. Hatred and judgment happen at a distance, but it is much harder to hate and criticize up close and personal. We fear what we do not know, and once we get to know the other then the fear subsides and we begin to realize that we have much more in common than what separates us. This program attracts inmates that typically will not come to other programs. POPP gets to the other eighty percent, the non program guys, because the project has teeth, and it has an edge to it. It also engages the negative leaders who have the power to change an institution, and that's exactly what they are called to do.

Inmate Peer Facilitators: An Unintended Consequence

For the first year of the POPP programs in the prisons, we used free-world volunteers as facilitators. This worked well because most of these men, especially in the maximum security facilities, do not have regular visitation much anymore and they value their connection to the outside world. Also, they would typically behave better when they were around volunteers than when they were around officers and staff. However, one summer the warden at one institution made the decision to have an open call-out ahead of one of my trips back to Michigan. The men were encouraged to write a kite to their chaplain or counselor if they wanted to take part in the next POPP forty day project. It seemed like a good idea at the time, but we had no idea of the demand that was developing. It just so happened that the church that had provided our original volunteers in that area was giving their members the summer off from service work. Their prison volunteers had tripled since the Power of Peace Project was introduced and they were trying to make sure they did not burn them out. The call out list came back just prior to my return and over five hundred men had signed up for the POPP program. We were not prepared for these kinds of numbers. We were already short on volunteers and every man was promised that if they wanted in, then they could get in. So another unintended consequence emerged: we were forced to train inmates to facilitate the groups and the convicts would need to lead their own. It was a risk. Once again there were many questions: would they respect the peer facilitator? We did not want them to be called leaders, but rather "peer facilitators" so that we were not putting inmates over and under one another. Would the groups run smoothly without the free world volunteers facilitating them? Would we find that many of the men were just coming to see their free world friends? Yet again, we were amazed at the results. The groups were even more powerful when the men were charged to hold one another accountable to the process. They were honored and felt responsible. They began to own the program and come up with more ideas and improvements. They respectfully challenged one another, and the older inmates began to lead the younger ones; and the younger ones began to show respect to their elders, which is unheard of in many prisons where the inmates are getting younger and younger.

Interestingly, some members of the community had predicted that the program would be less effective and unmanageable without free-world volunteers there to direct it. Well, they happened to be wrong. The program had found a new fuel and power behind it now, and the groups came together even more. They were proving a point: if they were trusted and somewhat empowered, then they would act more civilized and their behavior would improve. That flies in the face of the general assumptions out there about convicts. If they are treated like they are untrustworthy, unmanageable, and uncontainable, then more times than not they will tend to live up to or down to what is expected of them. The same thing happens in the outside world: people will behave generally the way that you expect them to behave—at least around you they will. But give a man respect, a little bit of trust, and responsibility? He'll oftentimes impress you with his effort and follow through. I do believe there is still a place for Christian volunteers in the POPP program, as well as Muslim, Buddhist, Hindu, Hebrew, and Native American volunteers should they choose to participate. However, they all need to understand that this is the prisoners' program; we just get to watch.

CHAPTER 14
THE MARCH CONTINUES

I am sitting in a small diner in downtown Selma, Alabama in March 2015. I am walking distance from the Edmund Pettus Bridge where the civil rights marchers were turned around and beaten mercilessly by the police and an angry mob. I have come here to prepare and begin to plan our own fifty-four mile march from Selma to the steps of the Alabama State Capitol in Montgomery, but this time with a group of young white, black and Latino college students—the next generation carrying on Martin's dream. That first march, which they now refer to as "Bloody Sunday" on March 7, 1965, led to the third march that Dr. King led, while escorted by National Guard all the way to Montgomery. Those 3,200 marchers took almost a week to get there, but that trip was the catalyst that led to the Voting Rights Act being passed and the event that changed the Civil Rights Movement forever. I wanted to experience what they experienced and walk the sacred ground that they walked. Those marches, sit-ins, and bus rides changed the nation forever. I also plan on filling buses with at-risk youth and re-creating the Freedom Rides as we go to prisons where we will have POPP inmates inspire change in young minds.

These marchers and freedom riders were young people of all colors fighting for freedom. Just recently I added my name to the list forever on the "Wall of Tolerance" at the Civil Rights Memorial in Montgomery that honors and remembers the martyrs who were murdered in the Civil Rights Movement from 1954 to 1968. That is, those that we know of. Many more gave their lives so that this young generation can have a chance to do literally whatever their young minds can imagine.

As I drove from Montgomery toward Selma earlier that morning, and I was imagining that long walk, I was overwhelmed by the feeling that I should walk that same route, not only for the cause of freedom but also for the teenagers that were coming up that do not know about true peace. I began to wonder if I could get it done, as larger marches require permits, permission, law enforcement, police escorts, and I didn't know if I would be held to the same requirements. I was beginning to talk myself out of it. So, like so many other times in the past, I asked for a sign. I knew I would know it when I saw it, for He always seems to do that for me. So I continued on to Selma. As I drove across the Edmund Pettus Bridge that I had read about in civil rights history, I imagined those hundreds of protestors viscously attacked on just the other side. I decided that I would park and walk up on that historic bridge, and I found a spot and got out of my car. I walked up and over the Alabama River, and stood at the top of the Edmund Pettis Bridge. I took some time to reflect, meditate, and visualize the events that had unfolded there and the eventual march that would prove to be a turning point in the Struggle. I took some pictures and began to walk back down to the base of the bridge on the Selma side. That is the place where John Lewis and several other young civil rights leaders were beaten unconscious.

As I got to the bottom, I almost stepped on it. There it was, tattered and torn; the cover and binder ripped completely off of it. It looked weathered and as if it been run over by a car or two. But there it was, a Bible, and it was opened to my favorite book and my favorite passage: Mark 2:17. That was where Jesus had been challenged about the company that he kept: drunkards, swindlers, prostitutes, and sinners. He had said that it wasn't the healthy that needed a doctor but the sick, and then he went on to say in verse 22, that you cannot pour old wine into new wineskins. It was time to leave religion and embrace the heart of the law. I too have had my share of religious folks question and oppose me for the company I keep: murderers, robbers, thieves, and violent men. It is still true today: it's not the healthy who need a doctor, but the sick. So I picked up that weathered old Bible and took it home, and now it is a prized possession. I asked myself, who drops a bible and doesn't pick it up? Who throws a bible out a car window? Who left it there? I had my sign, and I would indeed be making that march from Selma to Montgomery, because "The March Continues." I had read that at the Civil Rights Memorial in Montgomery that morning, and even gotten a T-shirt, not even realizing it was speaking to me.

This young generation has never had their own peace movement, as a matter of fact most of them have never even seen one in their short lifetime. The young people I work with are more fearless, daring, and brilliant, but experiencing more psychological pressure than any other generation that proceeded them. They are not dealing with it very well, as many of us wouldn't either if we were in their shoes. They need something that will inspire them to dream and to become bigger and better than they can even imagine; that's what the young are supposed to do, rather than just hang out, bored, wasting more time. They have grown up with technology which is the new normal that my generation only saw on *Star Trek*. We could not have even imagined the smart phones, social media, YouTube, Google, texting, video games, headphones, iPads, and so many other devices which disconnect them from the human socialization that they need so badly. They are growing up for the first time in our human history without having learned the power of the spoken word. Everything gets shorter and shorter and their attention spans are growing more fragmented, and they are losing the art of focused attention—which is how we learn and develop our brains.

So we aim to give them a peace movement of their own. How about we march for them? What if I get a small group of white, black and Latino teens to march and show the world that Dr. King's dream still lives, and the young generation is about to carry it on? That was Dr. King's final wish: to institutionalize this nonviolent struggle. It turns out this energetic, brilliant, talented, socially-connected generation is poised and ready, and on the edge of their seats. All they need is to be called to action in a language that they understand. Let's begin to march again.

The York Women: 40 Days of Prayer Launched

For the first three years of the POPP in prisons in Georgia, Ohio, and Michigan, we had only utilized three of the POPP Phases: 40 Days of Peace, 40 Days of Power, and 40 Days of Freedom. There was a fourth phase in the series that I had only run in churches that is called 40 Days of Prayer. My motivation for writing it was to give the communities where the prisons and schools reside a way to come together in support of what the inmates and students were attempting to accomplish. I believe in prayer and my idea was to get several churches in an area to go through a forty day prayer project in concert with the peace projects that were going on inside the institutions in that area. I also believed that business and civic leaders in those churches would be able to eventually raise funding support so that we could offer the program free to participating schools and prisons, which had been my dream from the beginning. When I told the convicts that there were people in the free world in that community praying specifically for them and their success, it only gave them more power, focus and a bigger WHY. It also provided the added benefit of preparing the churches to be more willing to open their doors to returning prisoners upon their eventual release.

This is such a big piece of the puzzle. When a man or woman gets out of prison, the most important elements for creating a life that will allow them to stay free are a stable, healthy, and supportive living situation, a job, and a faith family if they desire one. Sadly, many times it is easier for them to find a good address and a job than it is to find a spiritual congregation who is willing to receive them; even though that is one of the common themes that run through all faith traditions. Once again, we fear what we do not know, and it is harder to hate or judge someone whom you have been earnestly praying for over the past forty days in a row. There is also a strong spiritual power that develops around that facility as a group of believers begin to focus loving energy and intention on those walls and those within. Ninety-seven percent of the men and women who are currently serving sentences inside US state prisons are coming home someday. It is not a matter of whether they are coming back, but rather in what condition they will return. So the 40 Days of Prayer was the project that would pave the way to prepare the community for support.

However, it has been harder than I anticipated to find churches that were interested, for one reason or another. Most churches have many programs in place already, and understandably it is difficult to find room for yet another. But maybe there was another way to use this small, powerful book. There is a women's prison in Nebraska that has a wonderful warden who is very program oriented. She heard about the 40 Days of Prayer and they contacted me with a request for more information. After much discussion it was decided that we would pilot the Prayer Project there at York Women's Correctional Facility—the only state prison for women in Nebraska.

Here's how the project works: there are seven new steps for forty days that the participants commit to. These are designed to help you get very specific about what you desire and develop habits around searching for answered prayers and finding evidence that your miracles are on their way. Many people pray and either do not get specific or forget to look for miracles throughout the day. The women wrote down ten very specific "Impossible Prayers" that they wished for their God, as they understood Him, to answer over the forty-day project. Then they began the first of forty daily devotionals all written around miraculous events in the Bible. We call these prayers "Impossible" because I encourage the ladies to write down things that they do not believe can happen without divine intervention. I ask them to get very specific and time-bind the goals and dreams that they are setting out to co-create and manifest over the six weeks. Though this happens to be a biblical phase of the overall project, it is fascinating to watch participants of different faiths willingly come together to focus on timeless and universal principals that are found in Christianity, Islam, Judaism, Hinduism, Buddhism, and Native American traditions. Once again, we focus on commonalities rather than differences.

You see, most inmates feel as though they have been hurt, disappointed and let down, by the system, by their families, by their friends, and especially by their God. In response they have stopped hoping, believing, or expecting good things, because they do not want to be hurt any more. If they don't hope for things then they will not be disappointed again. This project encourages these wounded sisters to do the very thing that they are afraid to do—to hope again. These courageous women began to write down scary prayers and things that they had not allowed themselves to wish for in a very long time, and some have never dreamed this big at all. We launched the program with a big revival type meeting and they signed the faith pledge all together on the same night. One of the powerful things about this project is that it is open to all faiths. I invite them to journey together and focus on what we all have in common with our faith traditions, for just forty days. I remind them that all three of the monotheistic religions trace their origin back to one man's faith: Abraham. So let us begin there. Christians, Muslims, and Jews unite in this project with no judgment and in unity to see if they can find miracles together; and what happens is magical.

I was very encouraged by the energy and excitement at the launch, but then I went back to Atlanta. I knew they would meet together every week in small groups and discuss the weekly questions, but I had no idea how it would go, as we had never tried it before. I did not have much contact with the volunteers or staff during the six weeks, and I planned my return. I called the warden and asked her if I could attend the 41st Day Celebration and graduation, and of course she said yes. But she asked a favor of me: could we keep my return visit a secret from the women? She wanted it to be a surprise and I thought it was a great idea and I gladly agreed. When I arrived at the prison that week, it was winter in Nebraska and there was some snow on the ground. I got through the front gate and the shake down and I was hurriedly snuck through the yard during the evening chow. It is difficult for a tall man, that is not an officer, to make it through a women's prison undetected by the residents, but they somehow pulled it off. They took me to the chapel where the event would be held and sequestered me in a small room in the back behind the stage. After what seemed like a long time, the women finally began entering the chapel and filling the room. There was good energy and I could hear the ladies laughing and talking and buzzing around. When they began the meeting, a volunteer greeted them and then asked if they would like to begin by sharing "Impossible Prayers" that had been answered during their 40 Days of Prayer project. I was in the back wondering if anyone would share, and if they even had anything to say. What happened next amazed me…

One by one the women stood up and shared their most personal and powerful testimonies. There is a completely different energy in a women's facility. It can still be quite dangerous and even brutal for those who live there, but they carry their emotions closer to the surface, and their wounds are fresher. One woman shared, "My dad has diabetes, and I have not been able to take care of him. He has lost his eyesight due to his illness and I have felt tremendous guilt over it. So I prayed that God would heal him." Then there was a pause and she said, "And God answered my prayer, my dad can see again!" The whole room burst into applause and they cheered their sister.

The next spoke up and said, "Because of my charges, my case, and my sentence, I have not had the right to see my only son. That has broken my heart, and the only thing that I have wanted is to get the judge to change his mind and allow visits from my son. So I put it on my miracles list, but I was afraid." Then there was a pause and she said, "And last week the judge overturned his decision, and my son came to visit me this past weekend!" They broke into applause again, and they all began to hug her. Meanwhile, I was in the back room, unseen and in tears. I had bowed to the ground on my knees and I was once again overwhelmed at what I was witnessing. More women shared miracle stories, and one inmate even shared how God had answered all ten of her specific prayers. These ladies were beginning to hope again.

After all the sharing and cheering and hugging and crying, the volunteer got up and made an announcement. He said, "Tonight you ladies are going to receive your POPP Certificates of Achievement, so we wanted to bring in a special guest. All the way from Atlanta, welcome Kit Cummings!" I came through the back room door and they look at me startled. Then they broke into applause and came and encouraged me. I was blown away at their excitement. These beautiful people behind all these walls are some of the most grateful folks you'll ever find. They have lost everything, so the smallest gestures are treasured. I got to share with them about the impact they were making in the free world, and then I presented them with their certificates. It was a magical evening, and they set the stage for 40 Days of Prayer to be unleashed in men's facilities going forward. They will always be the first 40 Days of Prayer grads in a prison facility, and it happened in the middle of the corn fields of Nebraska.

The significant result of this particular 40 Day phase of POPP is that it ties in the community and helps the inmates feel support and connection from the free-world. Whether they are Christian, Muslim, or Jewish, every one of these prisoners desires encouragement, prayers, and support from the community that has largely rejected and forgotten them. This phase does not happen at every institution, but it has been powerful where we have launched it. This phase also introduces *hope* back into the equation. Even the inmates that reach and fall short, or feel like their prayers go unanswered, began to experience a rekindling of their faith. Recently, over six hundred men in one Midwestern prison signed up for this phase—because hope is contagious.

Dexter and the Monumental Confession

I now believe that God is still in the miracle business and He is always doing His good work. We just need to show up and keep our eyes open, and get in position to witness it. That is exactly what happened one day in a prison in Georgia.

Many people ask me how these men are able to change in their current condition, and especially why the 40 Days of Prayer works so powerfully in a dangerous prison. They wrongly assume that men inside are not spiritual. The truth is that I see a hunger and spiritual intensity behind the wire that is rare in many churches. Many of these men are broken; they have hit rock bottom; they are grateful for anyone that comes inside trying to help them; they are fiercely loyal and their word counts; they treasure journals and Bibles and will stay and listen as long as you want to preach. There is a hunger and thirst for change there that is very special and rare. Pastors long for congregations that resemble what I have just mentioned. Here is a drastic example.

I am sitting in a gym in a prison far away, at a table with convicts who are trying to change their lives. This is a maximum security facility, and most of these men are doing long sentences (fifteen years or more, to life). This is an effective faith-based program called Kairos for which I was volunteering and doing some spokesperson work. There are seven tables of nine participants and free world volunteers. The event lasts from Thursday evening to Sunday afternoon, with fourteen hour days on Friday and Saturday. Lives are changed. I am there serving as clergy, so throughout the weekend if inmates need to "claim some time" and talk to someone who is qualified one on one, then there is a process to set that up. We have created a small chapel inside of the gym for such meetings to take place, where there is some privacy away from the crowd. I have had several of these intimate discussions throughout the weekend, but one stands out among the others and it is one that I will never forget.

A man named Dexter asks to speak with me and we walk over to the private area. He is tall and thin, he's well into his fifties, and he's been down seventeen years. He is visibly shaken as though something has been bothering him more and more as the weekend has progressed. He says he can't take it anymore and he needs to get it out. He is burdened and weary, and his eyes begin to fill with tears. I ask him what his motivation is: did he just want to clear his conscious? Did he want to try and get right with God?

Did he have a problem with another inmate that he needed help straightening out? He replied, "I need help with all of those, but none of that is what I came to you for." I told him that he was protected by my confidentiality as clergy and that he could speak freely. He told me that he had been carrying a secret for seventeen years and that it was killing him. He told me he had to tell the truth and bring it into the light.

He went on to tell me that he had taken a plea deal with the state to avoid the death penalty for the crimes that he had committed. He had been given a life sentence with no possibility of parole, and he said, "I am never going home, and I will die here. I have no more family to come and see me, write to me, or take my calls. This is my life and I have come to terms with that." I asked him if that was what he wanted to talk to me about and he said no, there was more. "I am here because I killed five people, and I can never take that back or make that right. I wish I could, but I can't." He paused for a moment or two, and then he went on. "But the heavy weight that I have been carrying all these years, and that no one else on the planet knows about, is that there is a sixth victim that I never got charged with, and that case has never been solved. All these years have gone by, and somewhere out there is a family that doesn't have answers and has no peace. I intend to change that." I stood there speechless. Here was a man, a killer, who was wanting to confess to a seventeen-year-old cold case murder, and he wanted me to help him bring closure to it with the authorities and the family involved. I didn't really know what to say next, as obviously this was new territory for me.

I reminded him that I was bound by confidentiality, and that I could not even be forced to testify regarding what he had shared with me. He stopped me and said, "You don't understand. I need for you to take what I said to the authorities. They can't give me any more time—I'll be here for the rest of my days. But there is a family out there that needs to know what happened to their loved one. I want to give them some peace." At this point he was crying. I went directly to the chaplain and that week I met with the authorities. They had me write it out, sign an affidavit, and make my statement. I let them handle it from there and I never heard of it again. The next time I saw Dexter there was more of a peace and lightness to him. He explained that for years he had been hard and distant, and back in the day, he was a very violent man in these prisons. But now, he just wanted to help people. He became a servant and his life changed. He prays for that family every day, and he is doing everything he can to make amends for doing the unthinkable and making a terrible decision that he can never take back. Prayer has the power to change lives, even for those who never need to be back in society ever again.

I learned somewhere along the way not to try to figure out who deserves help and who does not. If there is a line that separates those who deserve forgiveness and those who don't, then where is that line? Where does the last one of "the worthy" end, and where does the first of the unworthy ones begin. Does the murderer belong in the unworthy group? What if he killed the man who raped his daughter? Does the one convicted of a Ponzi scheme that swindled hundreds of millions of dollars from senior citizens belong on the worthy list? If so, how could that be for a person who wrecked thousands of lives? It is impossible for me to judge correctly and I am not the one who is supposed to judge anyway. So I just try to help anyone who wants help—and that means *anyone*, even Dexter.

Somewhere out there is a family that lost a loved one that they should have never lost. Nothing can bring them back, and nothing can ever take away their loss and pain. And I cannot even begin to imagine what that feels like or the deep sorrow that can never truly leave you. But somewhere out there, unseen in the darkness, is a man that prays for them every day and is doing his best to make living amends. Let God be the judge, and let us pray for mercy and grace for us all.

CHAPTER 15
INSIDE UKRAINE AND THE KGB

What in the world did I do to get myself into this situation? I am sitting in a state department building in downtown Lviv, Ukraine, and I am being questioned by men in uniforms and great big green hats, officials of the SBU, formerly known as the KGB when Ukraine was a part of the Soviet Union. They continue to tell me to wait, through an interpreter, as they speak to their bosses in Kiev. I am hanging on every word, though I can't understand Russian. I have been trying to get access into a Ukrainian prison all week, for that is why I flew all this way and what I had been promised that I would be able to do. I have planned to introduce the Power of Peace Project to prison number forty, and plant seeds to return again that spring to begin a phase of the program. Of course I would not be able to return the following spring, as Ukraine would erupt into a conflict and be on the verge of war with Russia, but this is just months before all of that transpired. He gets off the phone, and this is what I am told through my interpreter and pastor Vladimir: "They say they know who you are, and that they have been watching you long before you came to our country. They say they know what you do, that you write, speak, and make films. They have been following your Facebook, Twitter, and YouTube, and they know where your funding comes from. They say that you will not be permitted to enter any of our prisons on this trip because they are concerned about the stories you will write and film about upon your return to the United States. Kiev says that they will be watching you over the next year to see what you say about our country and our prison system. If you speak only well of our government, then perhaps we will let you work in our prisons on your next trip here. If you do not speak well of us, then we will not allow you to return and we will not allow Pastor Vladimir's churches to do their ministry in our prisons ever again. Now, you may go."

I left with my friend Leonid thinking, *Now that was fascinating*. Definitely something I had never experienced. But for Leonid, this was nothing. My older friend Leo, which is what I call him, is the one who brought me to this beautiful country. He grew up in Moscow and became a Christian there right in the middle of the Cold War when Russia was the Soviet Union, and the most powerful communist nation in the world. Leo didn't just go to an underground church, but he also developed an underground printing press and he printed Bibles, which he smuggled to underground Christians who were fighting for their faith under a Godless regime. He stayed just one step ahead of the KGB, and was interrogated by them several times. He is a true follower of Jesus in my book, as he literally put his life on the line for his faith. We became friends through a coincidence, or should I say, a divine appointment.

It all began with listening to an Earth, Wind, and Fire song on my headphones one day on YouTube. As I listened, a suggestion came up on the page for another YouTube video that it thought I would like. "Russia's Toughest Prisons" was all that it said. I didn't even watch the video, but just had a clear thought that said, *I gotta go there. I am going to go to a Russian prison*. That was it, just a clear thought and a firm intention. Within a couple of days, I received a call and an interesting request. I do a good bit of corporate motivational speaking, and I got this call from a stranger asking if I would be willing to help them. They were in a bind, as the speaker they had lined up had fallen ill and had to cancel at the last minute. They asked if I was available on short notice, and I quickly checked and it just so happened that I was. So we booked the gig for the following week. It was a wonderful event for professionals in the housing industry, and this was their annual awards banquet. It was a good-sized crowd, everyone was dressed nicely, and the energy was festive. I spoke for about forty-five minutes and somewhere in the message I spoke of my prison work, which typically is the case. It wasn't a big part of the presentation, but it was enough to get the attention of one man in the audience. Interestingly, he wasn't supposed to be there either. His son had asked him that very day if he would come with him. He told him that he had heard me speak before, and he thought that he would enjoy it, so he canceled his plans and there he was.

After the event, people began to line up for me to sign books and meet and greet. This small man that wasn't supposed to be there, stood in line to come and meet me. When he got to me, he introduced himself with a strong Russian accent, "My name is Leonid," and he said he had a question for me. "I would like to know if you would go with me to Russian prison," he asked. I was flabbergasted. He continued, "I cannot find any American that will go with me to Russian prison." I said, "Yes." He went on, "I do not think that you understand. I myself have never been in a Russian prison." I said, "YES." He began again and I interrupted him, "Yes, I have been praying that I would be able to go to Russian prisons. I will go with you." And there it was again—my sign. Leonid became my friend really quickly and he is one of the most beautiful, faithful, humble, and gentle souls that I have ever met. Two men who weren't even supposed to be in the same room that day, were brought together for a very specific reason. To preach to the weak and wounded, and to plant seeds for peace. So we went on our journey to the fascinating land of Ukraine.

I met with the captain that ran the facility and got to speak to his whole staff of administrators and officers. They were so hospitable, as he tried over and over to get me to share the customary vodka with him. Finally we agreed on coffee and chocolate in his office. They asked and I agreed to provide a gift from the Power of Peace Project of a window for their prayer room. The winters are so cold and harsh, and the broken window made it very difficult for the Ukrainian inmates to hold their meetings. It had been broken for some time and the prison did not have the funds to fix it. This was a good faith gesture of peace that I made in order to help the men in Prison 40 and to sow the seeds for my eventual return. The window was fixed and a part of that room was dedicated to the Power of Peace. I am very grateful and proud of that dedication. However, they would not allow me to work with their inmates yet, and as far as I know they could still be watching.

The Question of the Nobel Peace Prize

At a recent 41st Day Celebration in a prison in the Midwest, a convict asked me a question, and it is not the first time I've been asked this identical question. The young man, whom I had never met before, said, "Kit, do you think there is a Nobel Peace Prize in this for us?" I stood speechless and amazed. Just forty days ago these inmates who felt hated, feared, hopeless and forgotten, now actually had the thought that just maybe their work was worthy of the Nobel. I wondered if anybody in that whole state was having such a huge thought, or such a bold dream. How could someone go so far in just six short weeks? When being interviewed recently by a gentlemen who has worked as the head chaplain for the state of Georgia over the past twenty years, I recounted this story to him. He listened, then he paused, cleared his throat, and said simply, "My God." That's the power of peace. It transforms, it redeems, it restores, and it rehabilitates. If it can work here don't you believe it could work anywhere? This young inmate had spent just forty days studying quotes, working steps, completing challenges, working with a small group, and writing a paper on his Champion of Peace, and now he was seeing himself as an international peacemaker. I am proud to know him.

They need hope, just like the rest of us. I tell them of an experiment where a rat is placed in a five gallon bucket of water. The rat must swim for his life, and he is not built for swimming. The experiment is designed to see how long the rat can survive before it is exhausted and eventually sinks and drowns. The average length of time is approximately fifteen minutes. The second experiment is fascinating. Another rat and another bucket of water is used just the same as in the initial experiment, however, in this experiment they add just one more variable. The next rat is put into the water and it desperately swims for its rodent life. The difference? Every five minutes the rat is lifted out of the water for a short break. Not enough to rest, just enough to give him a short break before he is dropped into the water again. Hope has been introduced into the equation and the results are significantly different. The average length of time that the rat can now last has sky-rocketed to fifteen hours! Hope is a very valuable commodity. Though rare in prison and even feared, hope has the same life infusing power—it just needs to be introduced and the recipient gets hooked.

CHAPTER 16

WALKING WITH THE WOUNDED RESIDENTS OF FERGUSON

People keep telling me that this is not a good idea, that it would be dangerous. They told me the timing wasn't good, and that my type would not be accepted there in that place, especially not now, with all that was going on. But I feel like now is the exact time to go; any other time would make no sense. This is the right time, and this is the right place; and these are the exact people that I need to go and meet, and the exact people that I need to learn from. How would I know if I do not go? The nation has been in an uproar over the killing of a young black man named Michael Brown by a white officer named Darren Wilson in Ferguson, Missouri, just outside of East St. Louis. The country rioted over the Rodney King beating in Los Angeles almost twenty-five years ago, and then our nation was divided once again by the killing of Trayvon Martin in Florida just a few years ago. And with the Eric Garner and Freddie Gray cases closely following it, it exposed an ugly reality in our country that not much has changed, and that the racial divide is as deep as it's ever been. Everyone has an opinion and everyone is choosing sides, and most are not afraid to broadcast that opinion, though many know very little about that which they are arguing. They only believe what they have watched, read or listened to in the media, but they have not gone and seen for themselves. I think if you haven't walked a mile in the other's

115

shoes then it is better to listen and learn rather than preach. I have been guilty of that many times before.

So after I finished a series of events in a Kansas prison, I drove across the state line and headed for Ferguson. I didn't have much of a plan, but I felt a strong call pulling me. I've heard that voice many times before and simply followed it, and that has made all the difference. So I listened, and I drove. There had been recent protests and even riots in that community, where businesses were burned, looted and destroyed. It had gotten so bad at one point that the National Guard was called in and tear gas was used to disperse the angry crowds. I began to drive through St. Louis and on to Ferguson trying to find the exact spot where the killing had taken place just a few weeks earlier. The whole country was on edge over a grand jury decision as to whether they would charge the officer in the killing. I could sense the tension as I got deeper into the community. But I couldn't find the street, because I didn't know where I was going. How would I know if I didn't find someone to ask? So I saw a young man and a young woman sitting on a grass bank waiting on a bus. I pulled over and got out of my car. As I approached them they quickly noticed that I was not from around there. The young man happened to be black, and so was she. He had some fascinating artwork on his face and was wearing a Miami cap turned up and to the side. I asked a few short, but very important questions.

I asked, "Excuse me sir, can you help me?"

"Whatcha need?" he said.

"I need your advice," I replied.

"About what?" he said.

I went on, "I would like to get your opinion about something. I'd like to know what you believe the solution to this big mess is. I need to know from someone who lives here."

The whole vibe and energy of the situation quickly turned. Here I was, a white man that was obviously from out of town, walking around by myself asking questions to complete strangers in a neighborhood that was on the brink. He seemed to sense that I wasn't a cop, or a reporter, but perhaps just a friend. I politely approached, I called him sir, I asked for his help, and then I wanted his opinion, treating him as an authority. They were wonderful and offered a very articulate and reasonable opinion. Then I asked how I could find the place that I was looking for.

"You mean the hot spot?" he said.

"Yeah, I guess that is what I'm looking for."

He directed me, with a little grin, and then I gave him a street-hug. I said, "I got nothing but love for you man." And he said, "I love you too, sir." I got back in my car and headed to the hot spot.

As I drove down the street that had seen the rioting just days before, it looked like a war zone. Row after row of store fronts were boarded up, and the QuikTrip was burned to the ground, as well as other businesses all the way down that road. I stood in front of the stores and talked to people as they came out. I asked a young man where Michael Brown's apartments were, and he pointed up the street, "Just head that way, you'll see it." I walked on and eventually came to the spot. There was a makeshift memorial with flowers, teddy bears, balloons, candles and other loving gestures piled up in the street. There were also signs that had been propped up that read "Stop Killing Us" and other heartbroken messages. It was eerily quiet and deserted, and then slowly people began to come out and walk up to me. There I was, all alone wearing my "Hope is the New Dope" T-shirt and walking around the site and saying hello to anyone that approached me. I offered the same questions that had already worked: "Excuse me, can you help me? I need some advice and your opinion. What do you believe that the solution is here?" It was like magic. Before I knew it there was a small crowd around me and I was interviewing people. By the end of my visit to that tragic landmark, we were hugging and posing for group photos, with peace signs in the air—at the exact spot where Michael had been killed. Whatever your position is on that controversy, it's hard to argue with love. That picture is one of my prized possessions, and it reminds me that people are just people, and these were just heart broken, hurting families. They were beautiful and they treated me with nothing but love and respect. I wonder, who would have predicted any of that by just watching the news? I wonder.

The POPP Process: Part Five—The Champions of Peace Paper

When we get close enough to see the "other side," then we begin to see that we all share similar stories, but ones that are wrapped in different covers. There is a particular prison gang that is heavily entrenched in the US correctional system. They are deeply respected behind the wire. They grew rapidly decades ago as a way to protect inmates of a certain race inside state prisons across the country. They are one of the most feared criminal organizations operating on the inside, and they are known far and wide for their violent retaliations and strong arm tactics.

I have gotten to know a man inside a prison in Ohio who has been locked up for over thirty years. He has done hard time for decades and been shipped from one prison to another. He happens to be the leader of this notorious gang in the prison where I met him. He was invited personally by the warden to come to the Power of Peace Project when we rolled through this facility, because of his influence. He came because he was curious, and because he is tired: tired of the time, tired of the fighting, and tired of the game. He's a fairly large man, covered with tats. He has long hair, and a long beard, and horn rimmed glasses. He bears the scars of many years of incarceration, and it appears obvious that someone once tried to bite his nose off. He has pain in his eyes, pain that overshadows the prejudice that he has lived with for a very long time.

He came to me at the recent POPP graduation ceremony at this institution before he was set to speak to the men. He had been chosen as the representative from his family table to share what they had learned together on this forty day journey. He had his 40 Days of Freedom journal in his hand and he gave it to me. "I want you to have this," he said. "I want you to share it with the kids in the free world." I tried to refuse, telling him that it was his to keep and that it must be very special to him. He wouldn't let me give it back, and then he went and sat down. When it was his turn, he made his way to the stage and stood silent at the podium. Tears began to fill his eyes and he choked them back, making a joke that he was experiencing heartburn. All the men laughed, because they knew who he was. They call him by his well-known nickname, for he has spent many years building his reputation in prisons just like this one. You aren't supposed to cry in a place like this, and he was doing something he had never done publicly before: share his feelings with other convicts, even his enemies. The men encouraged him to continue. He pointed over at his table and said, "Forty days ago we would hardly sit together, much less share our hearts. But just six weeks later, I can say that we have become a family, and these men have changed me." He was pointing over to a table where there were seated black men and white men—a table that he would not have shared space with just forty days earlier. I was witnessing another miracle.

I took that journal back to Atlanta and I have begun to read his daily journal entries. It is fascinating. To look into a gang leader's heart and mind after thirty one years of the hardest time one can do, and to see his heart and mind being transformed...it is truly remarkable. He writes of his struggle to open his life up to other men and his fear of appearing weak. He shares of his decisions to order his men not to fight, and how turning the other cheek is something that he has never done in his entire life. He writes about accepting a daily challenge to sit and talk with someone that he would never *ever* have hung out with, and his decision to spend time one afternoon with one the most hated type of men in the prison, because of this man's particular crime. He shares very vulnerably about how badly he wanted to beat the life out of this man, and how the Power of Peace Project had turned him the other way; but how incredibly difficult that was for him. It is a rare peek into the life of another feared, hated, and forgotten man, and how this movement is changing him and giving him a newfound purpose for his life. A life that will probably never see the free world again. But perhaps he can be free on the inside? Freedom is indeed an inside job.

The Men of Ellsworth and the Latino Leader

The Champion of Peace paper is one of the prerequisites for graduation from the participants, and one of the highpoints of the project. Some of the men have to get help to write it, but we set the expectations clearly in the beginning of the program launch: if you do not come to all the meetings, if you do not refrain from violence over the next forty days, and if you do not make a sincere and honest effort on the paper writing project, then you will not receive a POPP certificate of achievement. All the men choose one of the twentieth century peacemakers that are featured in the 40 Day journals. We have chosen leaders from all the different faith traditions from around the world by design, as a way to attract men from all different races, cultures, and socioeconomic backgrounds. Hindus, Muslims, Jews, blacks, whites, Baptists, Catholics, Buddhists, Native American Chiefs, and Medicine Men—this is a program that attracts and engages all types of brothers, to bring their unique wisdom, courage, love and brotherhood to the circle, and we respect you there wherever you happen to be in your personal journey.

I went to a prison in Ellsworth, Kansas to launch 40 Days of Peace a couple of years ago. The reception was enthusiastic, as these men had heard about the program and were eager to attempt to bring about peace at their facility. We had the right men in the room, as well as some real heavy brothers with a lot of pull (in Kansas they call that "stroke," which means they carry considerable influence). After one of the sessions a young man came up and pulled me aside and said he needed some time with me. He said that God had been pulling on his heart throughout our two days together and he was ready to turn his life around and give it all to Him. I told him that I could take him to the chaplain, which I did, so that he could receive spiritual counseling.

This kid was all heart and no fear; he was hungry, eager, young, and ready to do whatever was expected of him no matter what the personal cost. He had been in a very well-known Latino gang for several years and now he was trying to pull away from that life, which can be very dangerous if you are not wise and careful, and then still it can cost you your life. His body was covered with the ink that represents his prison family, and so it was very obvious to which group he belonged. His particular organization keeps themselves apart from the rest and typically doesn't mingle with the other convicts. They are a difficult group to break into for volunteer organizations and it's almost impossible to get close enough to the leaders in order to win their trust and respect; and there is no way that you will gain the support of the leadership if they do not respect you. I had tried at different times in other prisons to find the right Latino leader to get behind the movement, but rarely had much success working with this particular group.

However, I never had a young brother like Ricky. He went to the number one guy and asked respectfully if he would join him at the Power of Peace Project so that he would know what his little brother was getting into. That took guts, because many times when you try to leave or radically change from that way of life and what they have come to expect, then you find yourself in serious danger. But Ricky sincerely wanted his leader to come, and to my surprise on that second day I looked out and saw a whole row filled with the brothers from this chain-gang Latino Family and his leader, the most powerful guy right in the middle. It was very impressive that young Ricky had recruited that group to come, because that is very rare in the prison world with the Latino gangs. In most parts of the country, they keep to themselves for the most part, unless they have a reason to get involved, and that usually turns out to be a bad day for whoever they're coming to see.

This leader is a very impressive man at Ellsworth, and I now count him as a friend and a man that I respect. He has done a long bid and he's learned how to do hard time, get what he needs, and how to lead an effective organization. His family is strong, unified and reflects the nature of their leader. He is always dressed tip-top with his shirt buttoned all the way up, his pants pressed and his shoes shined. He wears his hair short and has intense eyes and small wire framed glasses. The first time I met him, I knew

I was meeting someone of influence by the way that he carried himself, the words that he chose, the way he shook my hand firmly, and how he looked me straight in the eye when he addressed me. A very serious man, I got the impression that he was very smart, and a man not just physically strong, but also mentally sharp. Others had also told me about his reputation and what it had taken to reach his high rank, and that he was highly regarded by all the men at Ellsworth.

Over the forty day program he was chosen by the group to read his paper on his Champion of Peace at the graduation ceremony. As he walked toward the podium, I felt an interesting vibe running through the room, since he was a well-known brother of influence. He began by saying that he was going to be teaching about his C.O.P. (Champion of Peace), Mr. Nelson Mandela. He wrote five pages of some of the most powerful, eloquent, and inspiring words about this great man than I have ever heard. I was mesmerized by his use of the English language. It was if I were listening to a professional speaker, or better yet an orator, as he used beautiful words that rose to magnificent heights and then came back down for effect.

By the time he was done, all the brothers in the room immediately stood and cheered. That was the first time that I had ever seen a brother in blue receive a standing ovation from a room full of rivals and hardened convicts in a high security prison. That paper had been the vehicle for this man to show us his powerful gift and I was not only impressed, but also inspired. I have the unique privilege of receiving all of those papers after I leave one prison after another. They are treasures buried in a field, and they have been discovered and dug up; now it's time to dust them off and share them with the free world. I owe a lot to the Mighty Men of Ellsworth Correctional. They are faithful and they work hard at this project, even to this day, and I saw the true power of peace in that place.

Now Ricky is back in the free world. If he hadn't changed on the inside through the Power of Peace Project then he would have probably already gone back to the life that brought him into this system at such an early age.

That one brave and faithful move that he made with his leader will have lasting impact and maybe a greater ripple effect than he could have ever imagined. Who knows, maybe his leader could very well pull that whole place together, and we may never know. He has been trained and prepared all of these years for such a time as this. Why not him, and why not now? I have won the respect of a powerful leader in the Latino prison families, and God only knows what might come of that. We cannot have lasting peace in these tough state prisons without our brown brothers helping us, for they are a formidable force and their numbers are growing rapidly. In this fight, it is all-for-one and one-for-all, for this peace is too much for any one group to forge or bear alone.

CHAPTER 17
TIMES SQUARE AND
THE NEW ISRAELITES

Times Square. I love being here, especially at night; it is electric. I am here rolling through on a short speaking tour in Philadelphia, New York, and Jersey City. As I walk among the crowds, a platform with lots of activity gets my attention. It looks like a scene out of *Star Wars*: great big men dressed in elaborate costumes and preaching loudly over a megaphone. I have never seen this group before, nor have I even heard of them, though now I understand that they are well-known by many. They go by the name of the New Israelites. I stop and listen for a moment and then keep walking, fascinated by what I am seeing and hearing. They are gathered in groups on several busy Times Square street corners, and another gathering of black costumes draws my attention. I wander over and begin to listen again. This time I am mesmerized as I walk in closer and closer, until I am completely surrounded by the group that is listening to the large man in the middle who is preaching. I notice the signs that are being held up and the radical messages that are raised high. The message being shouted is angry in nature. There is a graphic picture of the twin towers falling and engulfed in flames, and there are posters about "American Christians." I don't happen to notice that I definitely stand out in the small crowd that is growing in numbers around me. I am caught up in the present moment and unaware of the situation that is developing.

All of the sudden the preacher on the loud speaker singles me out: "Why, there is one right there." He points at me, and a bright spot light is immediately directed at my face. I snap back to reality and notice that all eyes are on me. "Let's ask him what he thinks," he continues, "Do you think America should burn, white man?" Everyone is waiting on my reply.

I speak up loudly, "No, I do not."

"Why not?" he says in a very defiant tone.

"It probably has something to do with my work," I say. "I go into prisons, poor communities, and inner city schools, and help minorities and people who are oppressed to get out, stay out, and be free."

He is speechless. After an awkward and uncomfortable period of silence, which feels like a very long time, he replies: "Well, it seems as if we have found ourselves an objective one." He turns his attention off of me, and the light is shined back on him.

As I make my way carefully through the crowd, I am compelled to offer one more thing. I say in a very loud voice, and from the bottom of my heart, "I love *all* people, especially beautiful people of color." And I walk on about my business.

As I walk among the hustle and bustle I am processing everything that just transpired, because it all happened so quickly and I didn't really have time to think. As I cross a side street, I feel a presence, but I know a friend of mine is in the vicinity somewhere nearby. I walk a little faster, and start to feel as though I am being followed. I glance to my right and notice that there is a very tall man following close behind. I take a left and he turns with me, getting even closer. I walk across another street as the crosswalk sign turns red. Now he is on me tight, and I know that it's not a coincidence. My heart begins to beat faster, as adrenaline rushes through my body. I am now positive that I have a "tail." I decide that I need to face him, so I whirl around and look him in the eye. He is surprised and stops and just stares at me. He looks a little unstable, unpredictable. I am surrounded by people, and then my buddy, who I haven't seen since this whole episode began, steps out of nowhere and says, "Is there a problem man?" I try to appear confident, but my heart is about to leap out of my chest. The tall, angry man looks at me for an uncomfortably long period of time, and then backs up into the street. A cab stops and honks his horn at him, and then he disappears into the crowd on Time Square. Obviously he did not like what I said, or the fact that I stumped the preacher; or they had just sent him to deal with me. Either way, it could have turned out much differently than it did, and I'm just glad that I had a friend watching my back. It always seems as if I do.

The Fist and the Peace Sign

I often wonder what draws and attracts people to organizations that feed on hatred and separatism, rather than unity and love. It is an interesting human phenomenon: the longing to attach and belong. I have a fairly unique perspective as I work with literally all types of individuals in these different institutions. Whether it be inside prisons or outside in our communities, people are looking to belong to something. It can be with a radical anti-American organization in Times Square or at a country club in the suburbs, but we all just want to belong somewhere. Deep down we know that we were created to live in community and we will go to great lengths to find it. People are also looking for a cause to believe in, whether they know it or not. Without a noble cause, they will be attracted to whatever gets and holds their valuable attention.

I believe that this young generation is more distracted, disconnected, and disengaged than any who have come before them. It's not that I think them to be less intelligent or less talented; I happen to think that they are more gifted and brilliant than any who have preceded them. However, I think that while today's youth are under extreme pressure to perform, fit in, and succeed, that many of them are extremely bored and becoming increasingly apathetic—and apathy is much more dangerous than it appears. We have a generation that is losing its heart to feel.

Recently we lost a beautiful, young graduate of our POPP Teen program to a heroin overdose. Her friends took her to the hospital, dropped her off at the front doors, and sped away. She was gone by the time the paramedics found her. This young generation is hurting, and they are choosing to medicate and become numb instead of dealing with the root of the pain. We lost another wonderful soul, and we cannot afford to keep this uncomfortable subject under wraps any longer.

My parent's generation had the Civil Rights Movement; then there was the anti-war and free love movements; then black power and women's rights; and so on. But then a shift took place and the country began to get more and more self-consumed. This generation is more the "me generation" than ever before. With Instagram, Snapchat, Twitter, and other social media applications, anyone can become a virtual celebrity. Anyone, regardless of who you are or where you come from, can create a profile, take a fashion pic, make their own little video go viral, or even make their own sex tape—just like they see the rock stars and divas doing. They've begun to believe the lie that it's all about them.

They need a movement that's all their own, and one that can change their world. They need a peace movement that is by them and for them. This generation is going to be the one that changes it all, and I mean that and absolutely believe it. They are mastering the technology that is connecting the world in such a way that when peace hits a tipping point, they are going to make it go viral. They are brilliant, talented and in line to be world changers. They just need a glorious purpose, and the Power of Peace gives them that. It has darkness and light; despair and hope; it's edgy *and* it's cool at the same time. It speaks to them in a language that they can understand, yet it is built on the timeless, universal laws and principles of twentieth century peacemakers that they have not yet learned about. I recently asked an audience of teenagers if they felt that Mahatma Gandhi was a weak man. Several of them shouted, "Who?" I asked if they thought Dr. King was soft, and for the first time ever, I heard more than one yell back, "Yeah!" I was appalled. Here was a group of young people that didn't have a clue about who these giants really were. How will young ones truly ever know if there is no one to teach them, and how will they receive wisdom if there is no one to dispense it? They are growing up learning about athletes, celebrities, and rock stars and missing out on the fascinating history that changed the world in which they live. It is high time that someone teaches them about real heroes.

When creating a logo for the movement, I was tasked with trying to communicate these essential ideals and goals in a way that was honest, powerful, and culturally relevant to both this new generation and the old. I wanted it to speak to peace, but also be bold. I wanted it to be edgy, but not militant. I wanted it to be something that kids would feel cool wearing, but also have a strong positive message, and I think we nailed it. We have a fist grasping an edgy, forty day peace sign and holding it up high. It communicates several different subtle, but strong messages: "You must find peace, grab it, hold on to it, hang on tight, never letting it go, while lifting it up, and offering it to others." I love it, and so do these kids.

Our trademark has become selfie shots with peace signs that we take at the school events that we put on around the country. At the end of the show, all the students gather together in the gym or auditorium and we have a teacher take a big, wide shot. On the count of three all the kids shout together and in unison, "Hope is the New Dope!" and they raise their fists in the air triumphantly. We blast those pics on social media, and the kids follow, feeling as if they are true celebrities, but this time rock stars for peace.

Now we have an app that they can download onto their mobile devices so that they can take the forty day peace challenge wherever they are, and it can now become a viral peace movement. They love the pictures of their "Hope is the New Dope" anthem. And so do I. This is a movement that they can call their own: for teens, by teens. Let young freedom ring.

CHAPTER 18
DEEP INSIDE A HONDURAN PRISON

As I walk through the massive gate, I look up and see guards standing above the walls with M-16s over their shoulders. It looks like a huge village, with a network of shops, trails, and a mass of humanity packed on top of one another. I quickly realize that there are no officers to be seen, anywhere. This is unlike any prison I've ever been in. All the inmates are wearing their own clothes, whatever they happened to be arrested in. There are no assigned cells, just areas that they call "the caves" and each man fends for himself. If you're not strong enough to keep your spot, then you lose it. There is no chow hall, because the government does not feed them. If you don't have family sending you food in from the outside, then you don't eat; or you have to owe somebody, which is a very dangerous thing inside prisons. There are no inmate numbers, no state issued uniforms, no shoes, or boots, while some are barefoot or wearing homemade sandals or flip flops. Over 60 percent of them have never been convicted of a crime, but simply charged by the government, and so they simply wait and are forced to live in a place that nobody would ever want to be. This is a small society, a civilization inside these walls, where the convicts rule themselves. They have a strict code that they live by, and street rules are enforced by the governing powers that be. Everyone is aware of who runs things in this fascinating place. I was informed that if I could find the make-shift prison store, then I would know the man with the most power in this Federal Honduran prison, and I did indeed meet that man.

I am escorted by a trustee convict, and once again I am with my friend Johnny Moffitt. After we pass through the second gate, we are on our own.

It is night time and I stand out as an American and a free world volunteer. I am carrying a cell phone and taking pictures and videos, as I am told that they don't care if I take it in—a first in all of the prisons that I have been in. As I draw stares walking through this crowded marketplace, I give the familiar nod and make eye contact and gesture respectfully, as I have learned to do with potentially dangerous convicts and people on the streets in different parts of the world. I motion to them asking without words if they mind that I take pictures, and some shake their heads with approval, while some do not. I do not want to disrespect anyone, or make any of these men feel less than. We make our way back to the Caves and there is a curtain which separates these homemade cells from the rest of the space. They are stacked seven high and each man has a small cubby hole where he lives. I am surprised that they allow me to go in, and just as surprised that I am willing to go. The looks I get in there are not ones of judgment or hatred, but more of surprise that someone who looks like me has ventured this deep into their turf. I have no agenda other than fascination and curiosity.

As we begin to set up deep in the middle of this fascinating place, I notice women and children walking around. This confuses me, as I am not used to seeing families in any place other than visitation rooms in US facilities. I ask my interpreter about this and he explains that wives and children are free to come inside, and that this is the only way many of these men survive, as their families bring them food and clothing. A beautiful woman walks right in front of me and nobody even glances at her. I am astonished, because I can only imagine what would happen in a maximum security prison in our country if the same thing occurred. Inquiring again, I am told that nobody would dare bother that woman because of who she is married to. If you disrespected her then you would have real problems.

As we are speaking, suddenly the strong smell of marijuana comes into my awareness and I look to my right to see a man smoking a blunt right out in the open. Nobody seems to care and I remember that there are no guards present, so why should they? As we begin to preach the beautiful young lady that had passed by me earlier now sits down in the back of the crowd and begins to breastfeed her baby, while her man sits right by her side. I am definitely a long way from home. They listen intently for as long as we wish to speak, and then they graciously thank us and say goodbye as we leave. The small crowd disperses and they go back to what they were doing before we arrived.

As we come back through that huge gate onto the street, we gather and talk about all that we have experienced that day. There is a wonderful, older female volunteer that has accompanied us. She doesn't speak English and she is walking toward the taxi stand. We ask through our translator if we can give her a ride back to her home, and she quickly refuses. We ask again, and again she politely declines. We press a third time and she says no rather sternly. When asked why, she hesitates trying to find the words, and in Spanish she replies, "If you take me to the neighborhood where I live, there is only one way in and one way out. If they see Americans in the car, the gangs will shoot the car up before we can even get to my house. No, you cannot drive me home for you will not make it back." I thank her and remind myself where we are and what these beautiful people live with every day. Young people are growing up in their country raised by the gangs and becoming street warriors before they even have the chance to choose.

This is such a lovely part of the world with the most beautiful people that you will find. It also happens to be very poor and needy. Unfortunately, it has become a pipeline for drugs and gangs that are coming to America. Over half of the prisoners that I saw in the seven prisons that I toured have not been convicted of a crime, but only charged. They are waiting for a trial in desperate conditions, sometimes for years and years. Many are going in for gang related crimes, because of the gang war that has been going on in El Salvador and Honduras for decades. Many have forgotten why they began fighting in the first place, as they have simply been born into it. This is why I wanted to go there—

to learn about this fascinating culture from the inside; and on this trip, I learned quite a bit.

The Pipeline from Schools to Prisons

There is a pipeline developing in our country as well, creating a dangerous trend. More and more kids are dropping out of school and hitting the streets. One out of four will decide that school is not for them and drop out, check out, and disconnect from the main stream. This is not just an inner city poor problem anymore; now it is spreading out to the suburbs and middle class neighborhoods, and even the private schools of the affluent are experiencing these same problems. Addiction, overdose, incarceration, and suicide are skyrocketing, and the first step is failing out or dropping out, and never earning a diploma. A new phrase is developing that I am hearing more and more as I travel around the country doing this work: "Our schools are becoming a pipeline to the prisons." That ought to give us all a wakeup call and help us realize that the current system that is in place is not working. The system is in many ways built for young people to fail, and our youth are lining up to fill the prisons that we are building and investing in as a society.

The prisons are built in small towns where land is cheap and far from the large population centers where voters live, and oftentimes it is the biggest employer in that area and a very important part of their economy. Tough on crime platforms get politicians elected and keep them in office. The war on drugs fuels the system with younger and younger inmates who most times happen to be poor. Kids are getting locked up and being charged with new, mandatory minimum sentences. Unable to afford bail, families are forced to leave their kids in jail in a court system that is way behind and backed up, leaving those who have only been charged, but not yet convicted, there for eight to nine months at a time. Overworked and underpaid public defenders do not have the time nor the energy to vigorously defend a growing number of clients, and most cases are now being pled down and never going to trial at all—young defendants would rather take a shorter sentence than face the prospect of losing and getting more time. More prisons keep being built, and young people are beating the doors down to get in. They become young gladiators inside, and hit the streets again even more angry and violent than when they went in. A growing problem gets worse, and they reoffend and feed the system over and over: a repeat customer model and a revolving door system. It is time to change that broken model. The United States has five percent of the world's population, but twenty-five percent of the world's incarcerated. Our kids are also being born into this system much like those young men I met in Honduras. One way to change it is to begin to heal this cancer from within.

The POPP Steps: 40 Days to Power

As more and more people began to hear about the Power of Peace Project that was going on in the prisons, the more I began to be invited to speak in schools. Principals and teachers were desperate for help and the kids were fascinated with this story. So I began to develop a program that met some of their needs and touched their pain. As we moved into schools we needed something that the teachers would value and that fit the need, while providing solutions to the problems that they were encountering with their youth. That was what precipitated the development of the 40 Days of Power steps below. These again are a forty day commitment and signed by the students as a pledge in front of their peers and teachers. The POPP wristbands provide public accountability, and small groups help build the momentum. An interesting dance develops between the students and faculty as they all strive to live by these challenging principles for forty days in a row. The students respectfully remind the teachers of their pledge and the teachers challenge the teens to do the same. They have light-hearted fun with it, and a healthy bond is created with some, as together they try to break unhealthy habits:

1) I will not complain about anything or anyone; I will choose gratitude instead
2) I will not make excuses for my choices or poor behavior
3) I will not blame anyone or anything for my situation in life
4) I will not play the victim; I will take full responsibility for my actions
5) I will not prejudge people, situations, or opportunities; I will observe with fascination
6) When wrong I will promptly admit it and quickly make amends
7) I will treat all people the way that I wish to be treated

These steps directly affect our personal power. We live in a society where more and more people are playing the victim and avoiding personal responsibility and accountability for their actions. And our kids are watching. If you listen closely you will hear people excuse, complain, and blame throughout the day, so much so that many don't even realize that they are doing it. If I don't take responsibility then I lose the power to truly change—it will always be someone else's fault. I have parents, coaches, pastors, teachers, employers, and all sorts of other people in authority tell me that they love this as much for themselves as the young people that take the challenge. One pastor said with a laugh, "40 Days of Power? How about we start with 40 Minutes!" Well said.

An interesting dynamic develops while both the students and teachers are on this forty day project. The kids start looking for changes in each other, and teachers begin expecting better behavior from the students who wear the wristband. Imagine if we all made a commitment such as this one and seriously attempted to break these bad habits. There is nothing that couldn't be overcome. Blaming, excuse-making, complaining, and playing the victim are all habits of the weak and strategies for failure. I've seen hardened criminals and convicts trying to overcome complaining, challenging one another to not blame others for their choices, or make excuses for their behavior—things that are very challenging for those of us in the free world. They are holding one another accountable for taking responsibility for their own lives. That is where true change takes place and that is the power of this POPP program. I cannot expect them to do something that I am not willing to do, and if *they* can actually do it, then what excuse do we have in our communities? They are taking away our excuses.

CHAPTER 19

BIRDIE BOY AND THE SITUATION

We're on our way back from Jersey City after a successful New York, Philadelphia, New Jersey tour. I am riding with my good friend Gary, a.k.a. Birdie Boy, who has been working with me for the previous three years being trained for his inner city and re-entry ministry in one of the toughest parts of Atlanta. We are driving through the night and it is two o'clock in the morning. Gary is driving, which he likes to do on road trips and we are flying through Virginia. Gary happens to be an ex-con who has turned his life around after a short career in selling drugs, and he has now become a role model to men on the inside of what they can become when they get out. He has gotten his Master of Divinity degree and he is doing exceptionally well. However, he is a felon and lives by certain restrictions that come as a consequence of being convicted in the justice system. The car is black with dark, tinted windows and we both happen to be wearing all black. We are in the middle of nowhere, in the middle of the night, a white guy and a black guy, speeding down the highway, lost in deep conversation, which is our custom.

The time during which we made this trip was an interesting stretch. About six months earlier, I had gone through a very intense time. I had been working with a young man who was deep into a notorious gang where he had been a high ranking leader for a number of years. Now he was incarcerated and I was helping him turn his life around. He was awaiting trial on a very high profile case that could send him away for the rest of his life. His case had been made public and there was a lot of heat on him by some of his former associates as a result of his life change and some of the difficult decisions that he was making. There were threats on his life and he was being held in solitary confinement as a result. He was not weak, and was not afraid, and he did not choose to be segregated, but that was what he was dealing with. He had officers with him everywhere he went, and besides his mother and young children, I was his only visitation.

I had received a threat, by way of a text message on an illegal cell phone that he had been unaware of at the time. I was told in no uncertain terms, and with very graphic language, to stay away from him and to stop talking to him. This upset him greatly, as he did not know what was going on, and was very hurt when I was forced to withdraw from him for my own protection. It was a very hard decision that I had to make, and it broke my heart to pull away from my young friend who had become like a brother to me.

Because this case was very public, the gang task force in my county had sat me down and explained the risk—that they very well might try to get to the people that were close to him on the outside, which is what they are known for. I was instructed to take some basic martial arts, which I had done in the past, learn to pay more attention as I drive, what to do in case I was being followed, and to purchase a handgun and learn how to use it. This required obtaining a concealed and carry license through the State of Georgia which I did. This too was a tough decision, because I'm a peacemaker and this caused considerable internal conflict to carry a weapon in my car. However, I was persuaded by the authorities and my family, and I followed the instructions. This permit allowed me to legally conceal a firearm in my glove compartment when on the road in the State of Georgia, and other states where this license is legal. For several weeks a police car sat in our cul-de-sac in the afternoons just to keep an eye on our house and to protect my family in case anyone showed up looking for me.

So, months later we are driving through Virginia and I happened to have that gun in my glove compartment by mistake. You see Birdie Boy is not allowed to be in the presence of a firearm for any reason by law as a convicted felon, and he has no idea it is in there. The glove box is locked and I am in the passenger seat. All of the sudden, blue lights spin behind us and a colorful expletive leaps out of my mouth. Birdie calmly pulls the vehicle over, expecting that the worst thing that could happen would be a ticket, which wouldn't be the first time in all of our travels together. The officer gets out and walks to the passenger side and I roll down the window. The state trooper is young and seems a little jumpy. Tinted windows on a black car in the middle of the night doesn't help the situation. He looks in the car and sees the two of us wearing black and standing out because of our unlikely ethnic mix. He asked for my partner's license and registration and Birdie explains that it is not his car. He's as cool as a cucumber, because he has been in many situations like this before, which is the unfortunate reality of being a black man in this country and sometimes getting profiled. When the officer asks for my registration I suddenly realize the situation and that I have the handgun in my glove box, and the serious problem that I have created for my buddy in the driver seat. I freeze, not knowing what to do. I fumble over my words and try to think of how to best handle this very serious situation. I don't want Birdie Boy to go to jail, and so I stall, and tell him that I do not have it. He suggests that maybe it's in the glove compartment. I pause and say "I don't think it's in there, sir." The trooper gets a little more agitated and demands that I open the glove compartment. I reluctantly do so and then he sees it. He quickly places his hand on his weapon, backs away from the car, and asks us to slowly get out.

I cannot believe that I have accidentally gotten one of my best friends into this situation. We are placed against my trunk and he removes the firearm from my car and takes the bullets out of it. Then he calls for back up. This is excruciating and time stands still. It is freezing cold outside and we are stuck against the back of my car as the state trooper sits in his cruiser on his radio.

I turn to Birdie and say, "I think we're going to jail tonight buddy, and I'm *so* sorry."

He looks at me and replies, "*We* aren't going anywhere, but I think I am."

My heart sinks as I come to grips with the situation. We wait for what seems like an eternity, and two more Virginia state patrol cars pull in behind the young officer. A much older, more seasoned trooper, who happens to be the boss, steps up, and addresses me. "Alright Sir, I want the short version. Tell me what is going on here." I tell him very respectfully the predicament back home in Atlanta, and ask him if he has heard of the gang that is involved. His expression changes and he says yes, that of course he has. I tell him about my work and I let him know the specific instructions that were given by Atlanta law enforcement. I throw myself at his mercy and tell him that I am relatively new at this whole gun thing, but that it is registered, and I have a license to carry it.

He turns to Birdie boy and says, "I need an honest answer. First of all, are you aware that you are a convicted felon and what that means?"

"Yes sir, I do," he replies.

"Did you know that the gun was in there?" he asks sternly.

"No sir, I did not" Birdie says.

He tells us to go sit in the car and wait there until he comes back. He goes back to his patrol car and gets on his radio once again and we wait some more. He finally comes back and hands me my license. He informs us that he is giving me a pass, and to promise to leave the gun in the trunk until we get back to Atlanta, and not to touch it until the driver is no longer in my presence. I wholeheartedly agree. He looks at me seriously, reaches out his hand to shake mine, and says with respect and with a touch of gratitude, "Thank you for what you do, and keep up the good work, sir." He turns and leaves, and we slowly pull away. I turn to Gary and exclaim, "Man, we dodged a bullet tonight." He looked straight at me and said with a big smile, "I'm just glad I've got me a white boy."

The Lakewood Gift

Gary Burke began working with me in this field in 2012. He came from a tough neighborhood in Belle Glade, Florida and he grew up poor. He worked hard in school and athletics and eventually made his way to a small school in Alabama, where he played football and earned his undergraduate degree. He began to sell drugs while still in college and got hooked on the money as he traveled the country and dealt cocaine. That life would eventually catch up with him after he was married with four daughters, and he ended going away and doing a short stint at the Atlanta Federal Penitentiary. We met for the first time after he was released from prison, and we were both attending a church where I was preaching. We became fast friends, and I was impressed at the way he had turned his life around. He worked as a painter and handy man, and was a good father and husband to his wife and children who had faithfully waited for him to return home. Gary then made the honorable decision to earn his Master of Divinity degree from the McAfee School of Theology, one of the finest seminaries in the southeast. He dreamed of helping convicts turn their lives around in the same way that God had intervened and turned him from his former way of life.

Gary and I began working with the football team at Carver High School in an area known as Lakewood just south of downtown Atlanta. Lakewood sits right in the middle of the number one incarceration zip code in the State of Georgia and right down the road from the prison where Gary served time. Carver is a tough inner school where young men and women are constantly in danger of gangs, gun fire, crime, and violence in this poor but beautiful community of Lakewood. We began the Power of Peace Project during football season one year as a way to help the players stay focused, excel, and keep their minds on school and football and off the streets. During that season, two boys from Carver were shot down and killed on the streets of Atlanta. The players were affected, but they moved on so fast, as if this thing was quite common.

We had a contest for the team and we promised them that at the end of the season we would choose five players and take them on the trip of a lifetime. We chose the most improved, the coach's choice, the player's choice, the highest GPA, and the "All-Heart Award" winner. At the end of that season, after they made it all the way to the state playoffs, we selected the players and loaded them up in a van one Friday, and pulled out of Lakewood. Most of these boys had never been outside of the City of Atlanta, and they were now on our way to Washington, D.C.

My friend Melvyn Williams, who works with the Redskins, had set the trip up and that weekend was one of the best times of these young men's lives. They stayed in a nice hotel and ate at fine restaurants. They had good seats at the Cowboys vs. Redskins football game. They saw all the sites and even stopped by the White House. But the highlight was a recreation of Dr. King's "I Have a Dream" speech on the steps of the Lincoln Memorial. We had arranged for a friend of ours, Mr. Everett Darby, to deliver that famous speech impromptu on the same step that Martin preached from fifty years before. At the appointed time, I shouted to all the visitors at the memorial at the top of my voice, and we gathered a large crowd to sit down on the steps in front of Lincoln. Hundreds waited for us to begin, mistakenly believing that this was an official national park event. It was so powerful that the crowd demanded an encore and Everett delivered the Selma speech as well. At the end we introduced the Carver boys and the crowd gave them an ovation. It was a beautiful day.

Gary now pastors a beautiful church right in the heart of Lakewood. It sits right in between the Atlanta Federal Penitentiary and Carver High School. Quite fitting, don't you think? Birdie Boy is living his dream and he and his congregation are serving the least of these in that tough neighborhood. He is a living example and role model to all those convicts out there who dream of getting out and making a difference. He is living their dream until they can get out and join us. The Power of Peace Project wouldn't be what it is today if it hadn't been for Gary's partnership in those first few years. He provided me with credibility and respect from the prisoners and he vouched for me when I was earning my reputation with them. I am proud of Gary and I am so glad that he spread his wings and flew. Let it be so for many more who are still inside or on those streets. And by the way, Gary just happened to be that friend who had my back in Times Square.

The POPP Process: Part Six—Certificates of Achievement

For many of these inmates, when they are released, we are asking them to do something they have never done. Over half of them have never had what many would call a real job. Many of them come out of a cycle of generational poverty and have never even seen a parent go to work on a consistent basis. Most read on an average of a fourth to fifth grade level. When they get back into society, they face one of the toughest job markets that many of us have ever seen in our lifetime and they also have a felony on their record in every job interview. These men need to complete something, and to begin to build self-esteem and self-worth. The Power of Peace Certificate of Achievement does just that. These men value this document. Some hang it on their cell walls; others send it home to proud families; others take them before parole boards and judges; others will take them to job interviews and pastors.

I got a call from a gentleman about a year ago. He introduced himself and said that he served on the Georgia Board of Pardons and Paroles. This is a small but very important board of men and women charged with the overwhelming responsibility of deciding who goes home and how soon in the Georgia Department of Corrections. They have a charge that I cannot even fathom. They are tasked with protecting our communities, while also trying to decide when enough is enough and when it is time to send them back to society, and to their families. This man told me that they were looking at a particular inmate who was serving life without the possibility of parole. He said that they were considering downgrading his sentence to life with the possibility of parole, which is a very big difference to a convict. This gives them hope, and some light at the end of the tunnel, and it allows them to believe that at least it is possible that they could go home someday.

He said that the man they were looking at had told them that he was a part of the Power of Peace Project. He asked if I could vouch for this inmate and if he was indeed a part of the prison peace initiative. Also, he wanted to know my opinion of this man's character. I asked him his name and he told me. My heart sunk, as I did not know the gentleman to whom he was referring. Before we hung up, I asked if I could have his Georgia Corrections ID number, and told him that I would be happy to look him up and let him know if I recognized him. He agreed and I thanked him for his time. I quickly pulled out my laptop and went to the site where all the sixty thousand inmates in the Georgia system are kept, and I typed in his name and ID number. His mug shot popped up and the name literally jumped out of my mouth: "Chicago!" I was so encouraged. Not only was Chicago a member in good standing of the Power of Peace Project, but he had served faithfully as we had developed the prison peace initiative in the early stages. He would always be there early and stay late. He helped get inmates checked in at the sign-in table for our Peace at Hays meetings on Friday mornings. I called the Parole and Pardons board member back and told him that I not only knew him, but that as far as I knew, he was a man of respect with a good character and a servant's heart. He told me that they would definitely take that into account, and he thanked me for taking the time to check and call him back. I wonder if Chicago had any idea back in those early days when he was serving that he might very well be crafting his own eventual parole. We just never know.

Young Leaders Interrupted and Redirected

I witnessed a powerful 41st Day Celebration at a juvenile correctional facility in Ohio recently. When we launched the forty day peace project just eight weeks earlier, a couple of these boys stood out dramatically. One young man was definitely a leader, and he had the look of a kid who had been in the system for the better part of his young life. He sat in the same place each day and he had the same guys surrounding him all the time. People referred to him as "the Don" and he was the leader of a particular group from a big city in that state. He is currently serving a juvenile life sentence and he has made a name for himself over the time that he has been incarcerated. Unfortunately, he was one of the teens that I mentioned earlier that I felt was ready for the next level. He carried himself in a certain way and he was treated with a great deal of respect—actually more like fear than respect. At the end of the second day when I had the young men stand up and share about the specific dreams that they have for their lives, he ended his sharing with this: "I'm gonna give these forty days a chance, but on day forty-one, I challenge anybody in here to fight me." And then he stared around the room and smiled, while nobody laughed.

Just forty days later he was chosen by the staff to share at the POPP Graduation as one of the standout Power of Peace participants. I was actually very surprised to see him again, as I had heard that a small percentage of the boys had dropped off and either not continued or given half-hearted effort. Honestly, I didn't think that he would be at the graduation, but there he was. He came straight up to me, looked me in the eye, and said he was glad to see me again. I asked him to share just one story with me that was a powerful example of the power of peace at work over the past forty days. All he said was "Just wait until the ceremony," and then he grinned. He wasn't kidding.

We invited parents and family to the graduation celebration, and I didn't really know what to expect. Most of the men in the adult facilities no longer have family that are able to come and visit them anymore, or they simply choose not to. I wasn't sure if the same would be true at the juvenile facilities. But the families did come, many of them, and we filled the room with mothers, fathers, grandmothers and grandfathers, even little brothers and sisters. One of the other young men that was chosen to speak was also a natural leader. He has a genuine gift of charisma and magnetic energy. He was the kind of person who walks in the room and the temperature changes. That gift can be used to change the world, one way or another, and it was not a matter of if, but how he would choose to use it. These young men had been bitter rivals, and now they stood at the same podium together. Many times, day after day, they fought each other, and often they had been sent to the "hole" for violence between their two rival gangs. These two gangs are enemies because their teenage members come from different cities and naturally clique up with their own kind for protection. These two tough teens shared about their past with one another and all of the trouble and pain that they had caused their families, and both their mothers happened to be in the same room. It was a beautiful thing to watch these long-suffering, faithful moms being proud of their sons.

The first young man got up and spoke of the history between his former gang and their rivals at this institution. He went on to say that it would be hard for anyone to believe it, but that he and the Don had now become friends and right-hand men. They sat on the front row of the celebration dressed in white, cutting up with one another in full view of their peers, and it was obvious that they had become friends. I was reminded that these were just wounded boys and that their hearts were still free from many of the burdens and pain that I see in the men that have been locked up for many years in the penitentiaries where some of them are headed.

He began by apologizing publicly to his mother. He said, "I know I've caused you a lot of pain, and that I have been here a long time. I'm sorry for that Mama. And I want you to know that I am changing my life, and I'm gonna make it right. You don't have to worry about me anymore, because I'm gonna come home for good this time." He walked from behind the podium and went and swallowed his Mom up in a big, long hug. There wasn't a dry eye in the room and everyone broke out in applause. He said, "One thing I learned from the Power of Peace Project is that anything is possible. If I can dream it, then I am capable of achieving it. Who says I can't be a nurse one day, or even a preacher. Hmmm, imagine me a reverend. Has a nice ring to it, don't you think?" Everyone laughed and cheered. "Don't judge me on my past, for the past is history, and the future is a mystery. Today, I just hope you remember me. God bless you all."

When the second young man got up there was a nervous laughter among the boys. He confirmed that he and his former rival were not only friends now, but that they lived in the same unit together and went to one another for advice on important matters. They were now working together to bring peace to this small dysfunctional community. Was that not Dr. King's dream? He wanted to restore "Our Beloved Community." I often wonder and believe that Dr. King would have been so proud of these tough kids in these prisons now following his lead. I'm sure he most certainly is. The young man followed his partner's lead and went and hugged his mom as well. I was asked how something so powerful between these two rivals could happen in such a short amount of time.

I thought about it for a bit and this is my response: I think we give them something to strive for that doesn't cause them to lose their well-earned respect. They don't lose face or even lose any ground, but they are able to continue using their strength and leadership like they always have, but now for a noble cause. On this day they made their moms proud, they made their counselors proud, and they even made the warden cry at the podium. This forty day project gave them something to be proud of without making them feel or look weak. As a matter of fact, they came out of this program looking even stronger before their peers and followers, for now they were becoming like the giants: King, Gandhi, and Mandela. They had tasted, if even for a moment, true power; the power that comes from above. We want them to continue to lead, but just lead in another direction—toward peace. We call the greatness in them to come out and stand up for truth, instead of self. They've always wanted that—they were built for it—but they've bought into the lie and always just settled for less.

The teen who was chosen Most Valuable Player on this day by his counselors and peers was by all accounts the former "Most Violent Person." He came up to me afterward and told me that he was getting out soon, and that he would like to share at the next juvenile facility event in Cleveland as a guest speaker about his experience with the Power of Peace Project. I am so proud of this young man who has made such an impact in such a short amount of time, and that now he is even dreaming of helping others with his story. That's how you keep what you get: you just gotta keep giving it away. Recently, the numbers came in for the period of time that we ran the 40 Days of Peace at the juvenile correctional facility in Cleveland. They set a record in the state of Ohio for the lowest number of exclusion hours (segregation) ever in a month for the Department of Youth Services—that is a big deal as it means less and less juveniles are breaking the rules. Much credit was given to the Power of Peace Project—these young men are setting a new bar and making history.

This young man kept his promise. I recently got an email from him telling me that he was out in the free world, and living in Cleveland with his grandmother. He said that he was back in school and looking for a job. He reminded me that he still wanted to speak at our upcoming POPP program. Then he suddenly said that he had to go, "I'm texting you from class and my teacher is TRIPPIN!!" I told him that I would be honored if he spoke to his peers and that I was proud of him. Just keep giving it away.

CHAPTER 20
SAN QUENTIN AND THE OPEN GATE

I am driving across the Golden Gate Bridge in San Francisco and on my way up through the Napa wine country in Northern California. I am in this part of the country for a short speaking tour in Reno, Nevada and Sacramento. I am staying in San Francisco for the night, because I want to see Alcatraz again; such a fascinating history in that place. As I planned my trip out west, I did as I usually do: see if there are any special places in that part of the country that I want to see while I am on tour. The place that got my attention this time was infamous San Quentin Penitentiary. Known as one of the toughest prisons in our nation's history, I've always wanted to walk across that notorious prison yard and meet the men who are living there. So in the weeks prior to my trip, I began to put out feelers and work my contacts in the area, as I happen to know a number of people in and around corrections through prison ministries and non-profits whom I have worked with in the past. As it gets closer to my travel date, I continue to get the same reply: "You can't just get into a prison like San Quentin that easy. It is too short notice, and you need a gate pass which takes time. There are background checks, fingerprints, security issues, and badges, etc. Sorry, maybe next time when we have more time to prepare for your visit." I was disappointed and a bit discouraged, and I resigned myself to the fact that it would probably be another year.

On the morning that I was to leave San Francisco, I had a very clear thought: why not just go to San Quentin anyway? What could it hurt? I desired to get in, I had prayed about being able to get in, and it was on my way out of town. I would go there and if nothing else, at least I would see the view overlooking the bay through that famous prison gate. As I drove up in my rental car I looked and saw what I had only seen in pictures and in Dirty Harry movies. It was a beautiful, clear day and it was mid-morning as I parked the car and approached the gate. There was a booth there manned by an officer who had a very simple but important job: keep people in who aren't supposed to get out and keep people out who aren't supposed to get in. It was simple: if you had a badge or a gate pass, you cleared and went through to the sally port up the hill to get searched and scanned, only to have your ID credentials checked once again. If you didn't have a gate pass, you wouldn't even get a second look. I walked up, and the officer came out of his booth.

"Can I help you?" he said.

I replied, "Sir, I would like to enter."

He quickly said that he needed to see my ID and gate pass.

"I do not have one," I replied.

He said again, "How can I help you?"

And I said again, "Sir, I would like to enter." He looked quite dumbfounded and asked if I had an appointment.

"No."

He asked if anyone was expecting me.

"No."

He then asked, shaking his head, if I knew anyone there.

"No, I do not, sir," I replied.

"Look, I don't know what you want me to do, or why you are here, but I'm very busy, and if you don't have a gate pass then you're gonna have to move along."

I asked if he would mind calling someone about my arrival, and he asked who I expected him to call. While I was trying to think of a good answer, he offered, "Would you like for me to call the Chaplain?"

I said "Yes, please call the Chaplain" and he walked to the booth to make the call. No answer. He walked back looking a little relieved, and told me I had to leave now. I asked, "Would you please just try one more person?" Getting a little agitated he asked once again who I expected him to call, and again I stalled, trying to think of another idea. He spoke up again before I could respond, and said, "Would you like for me to call the other Chaplain?" I shook my head approvingly and he made the second call. I just did my best to continue looking like I was supposed to be there.

Now, on the other end of that second call was an empty Chaplain's office and a ringing phone. Right when the officer was about to hang up once again, a volunteer and former employee happened to walk by the office at just the right moment, stopped and went in, and picked up the phone. "Chaplain's office" he said, to which my new friend stated, and I quote: "Sir, there is a man down here saying that he has an appointment with you, and that he has come all the way from Atlanta." I have no idea why he said that, as I never claimed such a thing and I never told him that I had an appointment with anybody, because I didn't know anybody there! But that is what he said, and I shook my head in agreement once again. The volunteer hung up the phone and made the long walk down the hill to the front gate, probably wondering the whole way down how he could have forgotten an important appointment with a visitor from Georgia. He arrived at the gate after his long trip down the winding path overlooking the bay, and peered through the bars to see who I was and what I wanted. I handed him my card, told him who I was, and explained that I go into prisons, raise up role models, and give the inmates a voice to redirect the young generation that is lining up to get in there.

Very surprised, he looked at me with a strange expression and said, "I thought I was the only one doing that."

I replied, "And I thought I was the only one doing it!"

He exclaimed, "Well, you need to come right in."

And I said excitedly, "Well, that's why I'm here!"

It was rapid fire and we were both quite impressed. I walked through that gate, went deep into the heart of San Quentin, and walked through that infamous prison yard. There they were: convicts everywhere, playing basketball, lifting weights, playing cards, or just lying around sunning their prison tats. My facility escort and new best friend gathered a group of prisoners together and gave me the floor. I spoke to them about the Power of Peace Project and received a warm reception. I will never forget that day, when just the right person was walking by just the right office, and picked up a telephone at just the right time—an unseen, all-powerful, all-knowing, all-present, benevolent force was once again making a way.

POPP Foundations: Achievement, Reward, and Empowerment

What if I hadn't even bothered to go to the prison that morning? What if I'd given up, because nobody was able or willing to get me what I needed? I wonder how often we say we want something and even pray earnestly for it, only to give up because things don't go as we planned. But I did make the drive and I did show up, and that is when things began to change. However, I would not have even bothered if I didn't believe that there was a reward waiting for me on the other end.

One of the biggest keys to the success of the POPP movement in the prison system is that it is founded on the principles of empowerment, achievement and reward, rather than punishment. In the faith world many of us choose to believe in a God that loves to reward, forgive, and bless us, in spite of the mistakes and poor choices that we have made. We are taught the reward system in schools, sports, with our employers, and even socially. If we do well, we get rewarded. If we accomplish the goal, then we are compensated in one way or another. This is why capitalism works. It rewards those who are willing to pay the price for success, take a risk, and strive to not just compete, but to win. Corrections, by and large, has chosen a different path, and it is punitive justice.

The stats tell the story on how that has worked out: as a nation we imprison more people than any country in the history of the world and there isn't a close second; we are currently building more prisons than schools; for the first time in our nation's history the inmate population on average is twenty-five years old or younger; over half of those released from prison reoffend or get revoked within three years; two thirds of those entering the prison system are going in for nonviolent offenses, but the majority are being released having learned to live violently for survival on the inside; eighty to ninety percent of the criminal cases that send offenders to prison involve alcohol or drugs, but very few receive treatment while incarcerated, and are released still active in their addiction; mental health offenders often go un-medicated, and when they get in trouble they are often segregated from the general population, only making the symptoms worse. The more that violence and tension rises, education, programming, and treatment are taken away. So the men that need the most help rarely receive it, and the recidivism rate continues to climb.

Corrections has become big business as more and more prisons are becoming privatized, and the war on drugs provides a steady flow of younger and younger inmates that happen to be poor. The system is built on repeat customers to fuel a five billion dollar a year industry of goods and services; private investors look at recidivism rates to calculate whether or not their investment will earn a healthy return; and literacy scores for elementary school students are compiled to determine how many more prisons we need to build across the country. We know this: if our kids drop out of school, then we'd better get a bed ready for them soon…and a broken system continues to get worse.

I believe the answer lies in reward and incentive. I've seen that most inmates, when given the choice, will choose peace over violence and easy time over hard time. I believe that incentive works with the majority of offenders, and I know that reward is a much more powerful motivator than threat, punishment, and fear. The Power of Peace Project is built on the foundation that people are inherently good, and that they are made in the image and out of the same raw material as their Creator. Yes, free will gives us the choice to make some very bad decisions, but I still believe that people are good at their deepest core, even if we have to dig down very deep to find it. The nations that employ this method of incentive-based rehabilitation are seeing extremely low crime rates (Norway comes to mind). What would happen if we turned our prisons into treatment centers and universities? What if we spent billions on faith-based programs, addiction and recovery education, anger management, sex offender therapy, and mental health treatment, rather than building more and more prisons for repeat offenders? It costs more to incarcerate an individual in a high security prison than it does to send them to college for a year. The punishment for offenders is having to live there away from society and their families; there is no need to cause unnecessary pain, suffering, and brutality, and then expect them to be healthy and productive citizens upon their release. They are coming home untreated, uneducated, and unable to manage their own lives. There has to be a better way.

On my recent tour through juvenile corrections in Ohio, "MVP" rode with me all the way, and he did indeed speak at the POPP graduation. One thing happened on that trip that neither of us expected: NBC Cleveland Channel 3 did a story on him and ran it on the evening news. Now the whole world is learning about his change. I wonder if he had any idea how much things were changing for him when he was journaling in his cell all alone. You just never know.

CHAPTER 21
FIFTY-FOUR MILES IN FIFTY-FOUR HOURS

Recently the whole world was focused on Selma, Alabama and the fiftieth anniversary of the march that changed the Civil Rights Movement and proved to be the tipping point. President Obama spoke from the infamous Edmund Pettus Bridge and thousands ceremonially walked over the Alabama River arm-in-arm. But no one saw the tiny band of brothers marching that same historic stretch all the way to Montgomery just a week before. There were no camera crews nor blockades, no police escorts nor parades, no fanfare nor festivals. Just a small band of brothers walking through the rain, and through the pain, to show the world that this young generation has their own dream of freedom.

I learned so much on that three day journey, things I'll never forget. I marched with my son Cole and for his generation who are fighting to find their unique identity. He saw his dad fight for a worthy cause and he helped me along the way when I didn't think I could walk another step. I'm so proud of him and all that he is becoming, and I know that he is proud of his old man too. There were so many subtle life lessons learned along the way on our two and a half day, fifty-four mile march from Selma to Montgomery. After about the thirtieth mile, off road, along highway 80 in rural Alabama, I honestly didn't think I could continue, and the mental battle was intense. Here was the unheard conversation going on in my head: *You're probably pushing yourself too hard. You need to be smart here. You might be doing irreparable damage to your knee. Nobody would blame you if you quit. You've made it thirty miles. The rest of the team are young, healthy, and strong. Certainly they will understand. I think the pain is getting worse.* Blah, blah, blah.... But then I made a decision: quitting was not an option, no matter how hard it got, no matter what. Period.

My nineteen-year-old son told me after the fortieth mile that he was impressed. He said that he saw how much pain I was in and thought that I would be unable to continue after day two, and that he respected the fact that I was pushing through. That's all I needed to hear. Day three was miraculously different as we walked the final fourteen miles. There was a different energy in my body and the steps seemed lighter. When we got to Montgomery, I was overwhelmed with relief and gratitude. I know this might not seem like a huge physical accomplishment to some who are reading this, but we had just walked over 108,000 steps in fifty-four hours, and my trek was on ankles and knees that have seen eight surgeries, while fighting a significant unrepaired hernia. God taught me so much on that journey, and I got to walk it and learn it with my son. I'll never forget it and neither will he. At the rally on the steps of the Alabama State Capitol, he told me he was proud of me. That's what every father dreams that he'll hear from his boy someday. When pushed to the limit you find that you can do so much more than you could ever imagine, if you simply remove the word *quit* from your vocabulary.

However, there was something else that kept me going on this journey. Our oldest son, whom I wrote about in chapter two, was also marching with us. My wife Terrie raised two strong sons on her own, whom we are so proud of today: Justin and his younger brother Ben. She was a strong single mother who taught her sons to be tough and self-sufficient, because she didn't have a man to sufficiently help her when they were young. This is one of the many things that attracted me to her when we first met. She is beautiful, tiny, and full of life, but don't let her size fool you—she's a little warrior princess and she's fierce; and she loves her family like a mama bear. She is self-made and independent and her sons reflect her strength and strong sense of self. I love the fact that she doesn't take herself too seriously. She laughs loud, dances funny, and she happens to be the best cook I've ever met, and she's definitely one of the toughest women I've ever known.

It wasn't surprising when her oldest son chose to fight for his country when he became a young man. Justin was a good soldier and he's done a good bit of marching in his day: twelve years of service, four tours in the Middle East, and forty six months of combat, oh yes, he has done his fair share of marching. So obviously, Justin was the first call I made when I decided that we needed to take on the Selma March. He quickly said yes, but he said yes for a different reason. When he returned after his third and fourth tours in Iraq and Afghanistan, he had changed. We were concerned, because he was exhibiting the frightening signs of Post-Traumatic Stress Disorder. He had seen things that the brain is not built to see, and he had done things in the name of freedom that were hard to leave behind. He had lost good men under his charge, and he was dealing with a heavy burden when he got back to the "free world." Here is a staggering statistic: twenty-two veterans a day are taking their own lives in this country due to PTSD, addiction and various mental health issues. Justin made a decision to march for them and to give suffering veterans a voice that many of them feel that they do not have. Justin has gotten help over the last few years and now he is doing extremely well. He has a good profession, and he is a wonderful and committed father to our grandson. He marched those fifty-four miles for those twenty-two a day who largely go unnoticed.

Before we left for Selma, Justin made the decision to level the playing field, because he knew it was going to be quite a challenge for the old guy on the team. He chose to wear a fifty-four pound rucksack on his back, a pound for every mile, just to push himself. For all those miles he was always out front, and I never heard him complain. When we would stop for a break, just to rest for a minute, most times he would just keep going.

His shoulders almost bled from the weight of that sack and yet he never made excuses, and he never said a word.

When we arrived in Montgomery for the rally, I went up to speak to the small crowd that had gathered at the same spot that Dr. King had spoken fifty years ago when those 3,200 freedom fighters had arrived at that same historic place. On that day Dr. King delivered his famous "How Long, Not Long!" speech. I was honored and humbled to speak on that hallowed ground about the Power of Peace Movement, and the young ones who were being interrupted and redirected from addiction, overdose, incarceration, and suicide. I spoke of the convicts turned peacemakers, and I spoke of the next generation and how my son Cole, his friend Ralph, and my college intern Christopher had marched to carry the dream to their generation (young, black, white and Latino—just as we planned). Then I invited Justin up to speak, though he had not prepared any remarks. He just spoke from the heart and said, "I want to encourage anyone out there who has lost hope and is thinking that they don't have a way out to hang on. I want to tell you to hold on a little longer, because it gets better. It got better for me, although I could have been one of those twenty-two veterans a day who feel like they don't have another option. I almost gave up. So hang in there, because there is help on the way." His eyes filled with tears as did mine. My eyes are filled with tears as I write this.

I believe that there are many men on the inside that are battling some of those same demons and just need help in order to heal. If they could get the treatment that they need then they too might choose a better way. But we need to give them the help that they so desperately need. I also believe that we have a young generation who are reacting to a "new normal" that their young minds cannot handle in a healthy manner. They are responding in much the same way that the inmates and veterans are: shutting down, tuning out, medicating, and losing hope. They need a purpose, a big WHY, and healthy role models. Those role models are emerging in some very unlikely places.

Pride for the Families Back Home

Lack of purpose is the root of much trouble in the human existence. Where there is emptiness of purpose, the soul gets restless. When the soul gets restless, it will try to find a way to entertain itself, but will always be unable to fill the hole inside. One of things we teach in the prisons and the schools is that your WHY had better be bigger than your largest obstacle, your best excuse, and your greatest fear. If it isn't, then you will quit every time with no exceptions. Most of these men and women lack a noble purpose: a reason to get up in the morning, and something to dream about when they lie in bed at night. Actually, there are many people in the free world drifting aimlessly, uninspired, or bored because they lack a big WHY.

It is said that hope deferred makes the heart sick. The Power of Peace Project gives the hungry heart a noble purpose for forty days at a time—enough time to get hooked on hope. Families back home waiting patiently tend to be a good place to start when searching for a big why. They are the ones who have been left behind, taken for granted, or simply forgotten—especially the little ones who never had a choice. We aim to inspire fathers and mothers, and sons and daughters, to care about the loved ones who remain, even as they learn to care about themselves again. Most of these men and women have a trail of tears, wreckage, and broken bridges behind them. Some of their families have given up on them, or more likely they've just given up on themselves. Giving them a good reason is sometimes all it takes to begin the road back home.

The Anti-Virus

My friend Gary and I were riding through the middle of nowhere one day, coming back from another prison, and he said something that caught my attention and proved to be another turning point. He said, "What we do is kind of like an anti-virus." I asked him to explain. He said, "POPP is like the antivirus to an illness or disease." We began to flesh it out and it made so much sense. When you get a flu shot you actually receive a little bit of the flu virus. Your body builds immunity to the virus by getting some of the dead virus and developing antibodies around it, so that when the virus shows up again it knows how to defend itself against the attack. And anti-venoms are produced by poisoning animals with snake venom, which causes the animals' bodies to produce natural antibodies to fight the venom. This seems completely backwards, but it works. So we reasoned that if the flu is the answer to the flu, and venom is the cure for a snake bite, then what would be the solution to crime in our country? The answer was obvious: transformed criminals. They tore it up; why not ask them to go back and fix it up? It turns out that many of them do want to help and be a part of the solution, it just so happens that nobody has ever thought to ask them. All they need is a good reason, and for someone to believe in them and to send them back.

They are the solution to the problem and they need to be called to go back to their communities and raise their babies who have been selfishly left behind. These young men and women are being forced to raise themselves because the strong males in their neighborhoods are missing, and it's time for many of them to repent and return. POPP helps them believe that they can, and invites their families to begin to believe in them once again. Hope is quite a powerful thing, and it always works when it is added to the mix. What is the biggest problem POPP currently faces? Getting ready for the thousands of inmates who are going to be getting out and possibly calling us, wanting to help. I know this because a countless number of inmates tell me so on a regular basis and are already beginning to write. It's an army of transformed criminals being trained behind the wire. We better get ready for the next wave—the Antivirus is emerging.

CHAPTER 22
ABRAHAM AND SARAH IN THE PARK

I am walking through Centennial Park in downtown Atlanta. This park was built as a memorial to the 1996 Summer Olympics that were hosted here. I love my town Atlanta and I love this park. I enjoy wandering through it from time to time, and it makes me feel good every time I experience it again. However, this day is different. I am agitated, frustrated, discouraged, and a little depressed. This ministry that has chosen me and become my passion and great life's work brings opposition, conflict, suffering, and sometimes deep pain. But the trouble doesn't always necessarily come from the people who are in desperate trouble that I work with, for that side of the work brings me much joy and fulfillment. It's not the dangerous environments that my work takes me into, for that helps me feel alive, keeps me on the edge, and invigorates me. It's not the hectic pace, or the travel, or the sadness that comes from feeling people suffer, for that fills me with compassion and keeps me on purpose. It's not even the loneliness that sometimes accompanies this dream and this mission, as I spend hours on the road and nights alone in hotels away from my family.

The opposition stems from an unlikely place. My ministry to the least of these has pulled me away from faith-based work that is more mainstream. This "ministry of trouble" is hard to define, almost impossible to measure, and very hard to predict, and this has sometimes separated me from more traditional ministers. There is a distance that has developed from some of those that I used to be close to, who I still love, who I rarely see anymore. I felt as though I was forced to make a choice between traditional ministry and taking care of the converted, versus ministering to the least of these outside the safe confines of the church building. It also forced me to become open to other faith traditions, and to become all things to all men in order to win some. That was difficult at first, but I came to believe that was what God was calling me to do—to plant seeds which would grow and allow other programs to flourish and reap the harvest. But on this day, as I walk through the park, I am right in the middle of the internal battle, and it is heavy on my heart. I walk, and wrestle, and I pray, *What happened, Father? All I did was follow my heart and go where you told me to go, and do what you told me to do. Where have all my friends gone? Where is the support and partnership that I prayed for and expected? Where are all my partners when I need them most?* I was indignant, but filled with a bit of self-pity as well. I now see that I have made many mistakes, sometimes come on too strong, and run over people in my zeal, stubbornness, and passion. I have apologized and tried to make those things right, but I could never really get them back. So I walked, prayed, and wrestled some more, unaware of anything or anyone else around me in the park.

I looked up and suddenly saw two fascinating people walking toward me. They got my attention, because they were a striking couple. They appeared to be homeless, as I could tell by their tattered clothing, holes in their shoes, and weathered faces and hands. They were old and thin from hunger and the streets. The man had long unkempt hair that had formed into silver, natural dreadlocks. He had a long, tangled beard, and deep, worn grooves etched into his wise looking face. She was small and thin, and very meek. She looked as if the streets had been hard on her, but she also had a strength about her that was obvious. They looked right through me as we passed one another. I had a black T-shirt on that read,

"Eracism," that I had gotten at the Lorraine Motel where Dr. King was assassinated in Memphis.

As he passed he said softly, "I like your shirt, young man."

Not really hearing what he said I turned and said, "Excuse me?" He said it again and I thanked him. Now we were stopped and facing one another, so I extended my hand and introduced myself.

He said, "I am Abraham and this is Sarah."

I replied, "You're kidding, right? Abraham and Sarah? That's awesome."

He stood there without expression and continued, "I have something to tell you, young man." Startled, I asked him what it was. He went on, "Don't stop speaking about what you have seen and heard. Those who oppose you are just afraid. Keep doing what the Father has told you to do, and it'll be alright."

I was speechless. Sarah motioned and started to explain further, but as soon as she began to speak, Abraham raised his hand and put it on her shoulder and interrupted, "Sarah, he heard what I said." She became quiet, and just looked at me.

Then a question simply came to me. "Sir, were you sent here to give me this message?" I asked.

He looked deep into my eyes and replied, "Yes, I was." Then they turned and walked away.

As I was processing what had just happened, I was light-headed and a little confused. I turned and looked back and they were well on their way, and all I could see were their silhouettes in the distance. I never saw them again, but God had clearly sent me a message and once again given me a sign.

This wasn't my first or last encounter with angels. My daughter Laina and I are fascinated with angels and we search for them constantly. She loves the story of Abraham and Sarah in the park. She is the light of my life, and we have a special father-daughter relationship which I treasure. She loves to go on "Daddy Dates" and she will still hold hands with me in the mall, which is rare for a teenager. We have always had deep talks and no subject is off limits. I learn so much from her about what teenage girls are dealing with in this ever-changing culture, and what she shares with me is invaluable. I have learned in my work that much of the trouble that young women face has to do with the absent father. Young women are going through the change at an earlier age, struggling with alcohol and drugs, experimenting with sex, and becoming much more prone to being lured into risky and dangerous situations, most of which come from dad being gone or just "not there" emotionally for their little girls. You don't have to leave the house to be gone, though broken families and divorce have effected a whole generation of women. I see lots of pain in the prisons because fathers and mothers have been separated from their children, however, many families in the free world are just as disconnected from their children, and we as a society are losing touch with many of them.

Teens are angry and hurt and need their fathers. I could have been just another deadbeat dad, but God protected me from making the biggest mistake of my life: losing my kids. Of all the bad choices I made, I didn't make that one and I am forever grateful. Even after the divorce when they were young, I had them every weekend and we have always remained tight. My son and I talk almost every day. He seeks advice from me, we share similar interests and hobbies, and we even like the same music and movies. There is no other guy on the planet that I would rather spend time with than Cole. I recently cancelled a trip to Cuba for a prison event, because I had made very special plans with him and I refused to break them. I can go on other mission trips, but I wouldn't have ever been able to replace that special time. Nowadays the highlight of my week is seeing my beautiful daughter Laina, my little artist. I couldn't be any more proud of them and I couldn't ask for anything more. They are perfect to me. As they go through their storms in life they know they have an imperfect, flawed father who has been through the storms as well and can walk along with them; and they continue to allow me to. I will never be able to express how much that means to me.

My daughter and I have a game that we play. We look for angels and search for God's fingerprints every day. The first one to see an "angel sighting" takes a picture and sends it to the other. Because it is our personal adventure, I won't go into details, but we have discovered some amazing miracles together, and suffice it to say that we are surrounded by angels— I believe that literally. God is forever surrounding, protecting, connecting, restoring, redeeming, and healing. All we have to do is keep our eyes open, remain alert, and search for his fingerprints, for they are everywhere.

Sometimes angels are right next door and you may not even know it. I have a young friend at our church named Little Tony and he is twelve years old. This little boy has a particular condition which limits him in some areas but makes him extraordinary in many others. I am fortunate to spend time with him every now and then, and I get to be like a big brother to him. He is brilliant. I can talk to him about cosmology, physics, quantum mechanics, or brain science, and I often do. We walk around the park and converse on interesting subjects or share a pizza and discuss his latest idea for another invention he has been dreaming up. But that's not the most amazing thing about my little buddy Tony. It is his inability to lie that fascinates me the most. I don't think he would even understand the concept if someone tried to explain it to him, as it would be so foreign to him, and I don't think that it would even occur to him to try. He is the most honest and pure little boy that I have ever known. I wonder what the world would look like through the eyes of a boy who couldn't tell a lie. I would love to know what that depth of honesty feels like, as we live in a world where lying has become almost common place. I happen to think that he is an angel in disguise, hiding out down here in a little boy's body just watching us and guiding us every now and then as he is able. I love my little friend, Tony, and I see God's fingerprints all around him.

The POPP Process: Part Seven—The 41ˢᵗ Day Celebration

I happened to meet Abraham in the park exactly when I needed him. He had a specific and timely message tailored perfectly for my particular situation. All it took was a little bit of encouragement to get me going in the right direction again. It turns out that many of the men inside these prisons just need some inspiration and encouragement as well. They live in a place where they rarely if ever get rewarded, encouraged, or celebrated, and that can deeply wound the soul.

One of the big highlights of the forty day peace project is the 41st Day Celebration. I now understand what a big deal this is for these felons turned peacemakers. Many of them have never been applauded, at least not in a very long time. Many haven't heard the word congratulations in years, if ever. They have forgotten how good it feels when someone tells you that they are proud of you. But to watch them celebrate, reward, commend, and cheer one another is something I wish that you could see. The joy that comes, the dignity that is inspired, and the sense of accomplishment and pride that exudes from them is truly unforgettable. I have watched grown men cry in a place where everyone knows that is not supposed to happen. I have seen rivals and enemies hug and high five. I have seen men dance and sing in a place known for misery and pain. And I have seen men, some of whom have never accomplished anything significant in their lives, begin to come alive. The celebration takes on a life of its own, and every single one is unique and special.

I realize how many things I take for granted while in the free world when I go behind the wire. Men in blue look at pizza and say that they haven't had a treat like this in years. I don't even like pizza anymore, but I would if I was in there. I have seen men in white give a piece of fried chicken to a brother who didn't have any, and sometimes I see people in churches not willing to do that. I have also seen men eat more Italian sausage hotdogs than I would have believed is possible! Gratitude is a very powerful and transformative emotion, and these men have taught me to value the little things in life, and the things that I take for granted. The 41st Day Celebration is a very important part of the peace process. Because just for a minute, these men feel like they are in the free world again. It gives them just a little bit of hope in a place that steals and kills hope. They begin to treat each other, for a moment, the way they wish to be treated, and the way that they will need to treat people when they return to civilization. I treasure these celebrations, for it is the good stuff—stuff that I wish you could see for yourself.

The C.O.P. Dedication

Recently I was part of a POPP 41st Day Celebration that I will never forget. The celebrations are all so special and unique; each one is different from the next, because each forty day project reflects the individual participants and their unique journeys. The family tables develop their own identity, and the papers that the convicts write are always different depending on the unique perspective from which the story is being told. Leading up to the celebration, five men are chosen who have written stand-out papers on their Champions of Peace. While all the papers are special, we choose five standouts based on a diversity of black, white, Latino; Christian, Muslim, Jew, Native American, old and young. These men get up in front of their peers, rivals, and former enemies and share their journey patterned after one of the C.O.P. that they have studied together over the six week project.

On this particular occasion, a gentleman got up to the podium and pulled out his paper to address his brothers in blue. He was an older black man that had been locked up for over twenty-five years. He was highly respected and remarkably intelligent, though he was weathered from years of incarceration. He began by telling us all that he met his C.O.P. in 1999 when their paths first crossed at a prison called Mansfield in Ohio (the prison where *The Shawshank Redemption* was filmed). They would meet again in 2005 at a prison called Marion Correctional. He told the story of this man making a promise to his mother on her death bed about changing his life forever. After wrestling with that commitment for a number of years, the man finally kept his promise and changed his life for good. This older black man spoke eloquently about this man becoming his role model and how he had changed his life because of his positive example. He talked of their friendship, mutual admiration, and bond with one another throughout the years, as both of them served their life sentences. Both of these men are along in years now, well into their sixties, and they might never go home.

Nobody in the room, including myself, knew who this inmate was referring to until he came to the end of his paper. With tears in his eyes, he told the group that his Champion of Peace was his brother, who was sitting right there in the front row. As they both wept, he walked over and they hugged each other for what seemed like a very long time. These men have the same mother, and I happen to believe that she is watching over them and must be very proud. Even his brother, Luther, didn't know that he had been chosen as a Champion of Peace by this wise old convict. All these years they had served time together and now he was given a stage and an opportunity to tell the whole world about his best friend. The whole room stood and cheered, and most of us cried—grown men all of us.

CHAPTER 23
TUNNELS, WALLS, AND BRIDGES

A Divine Appointment in San Diego

In early 2016 I received a Facebook message from a man I had never met. We had heard of one another, but this was our first encounter. Someone I did not know had read one of my books and passed it along to him. It resonated, and he reached out. How many times have I had a thought that I should do something, but I moved on or talked myself out of it? This time was different: he made the call and it changed my life. He had been doing cutting-edge, front-lines work in Tijuana, Mexico, a beautiful city that has become one of the most dangerous in this part of the world. There is a new cartel that has come in and challenged the current one, and the result has been a spike in homicides, kidnappings, and violence, and tourism has all but disappeared. Americans are no longer crossing the busiest border crossing in the world, and the city is on edge. That border separates two very different worlds. On one side is San Diego, one of the prettiest cities in the world, and possibly the nicest place to live in the states. On the other side is the wild, wild west; the third world just forty-five minutes away. It makes for an amazing mission field: you can go down to Tijuana and work on the streets and in the prisons during the day, and drive back across and sleep in "Disneyland" at night.

On that first call we spent over an hour and quickly developed a connection, because we were doing very similar work, but in different places. He invited me to come out, and I quickly accepted. He graciously invited me to stay with them, and I did what I always do when someone asks me to stay: I politely declined. However, something nudged me, and

I reconsidered. I called him back and accepted. As a result of that one nudge, a friendship developed that continues to this day. Over the next ten months I was there eight times, each time joking that I had my own bedroom and had become a part of the family—but that is exactly what had happened: we were family. We crossed that border together forty times. Mexico changed my life and the course of my work forever. Jeff Wadstrom introduced me to a world I had not known, and I fell in love again, this time with beautiful Mexican fathers and mothers, sons and daughters, grandfathers and grandmothers, and brothers and sisters, as they embraced me. They were not what I expected them to be. Once again, my paradigm had shifted. Their culture is beautiful, their hospitality is generous, their families tight, and their parties festive. I didn't find a dangerous city, but rather a wonderful people, with beautiful customs, and a rich history. Please don't believe everything you see on the news. Remember, judgment happens at a distance; acceptance is up close and personal.

Uncovering the Tunnels That Hide Us

I was once told by a man connected to the cartels in Mexico that there are approximately 150 tunnels running under that long border that separates our two countries. I have no idea if that is true, but suffice it to say there are a lot of them. We can build bigger walls, but they'll just dig deeper tunnels. Now those tunnels are elaborate and sophisticated, and some are even air-conditioned. Some are big enough to drive a car through. We have our own "tunnels" too—tunnels that we dig to hide things we don't want others to see. Tunnels that hide who we really are, or how we are really doing. I constructed my own elaborate tunnels to keep people out when I was at my darkest point. The problem with tunnels is you can't dig them deep enough anymore. We live in a new and ever-expanding technology and information age where there are no more secrets. It's not IF things will be brought to light, but rather how soon. The only answer is the light. When we keep things buried, and in the dark, those things begin to die and take us with them, or they are exposed in ways that are much worse than just coming on up out of the tunnel. It's not so scary up here after all.

The Dark Side Is Fully Funded

While our country argues over who is going to pay for our expansive and expensive wall, the cartels have no trouble with passing bills or finding resources: the dark side is fully funded. And the bad guys are well funded on our side of the border as well.

Prison gangs are big business. A friend, and a former inmate in the California Correctional System, who was once a member of the notorious and dangerous Sureños gang, told me that when he ran a prison yard at Pelican Bay, they made $10,000 a week through drugs, weapons, extortion, robbery, and protection. He taught me things I did not know. He helped me understand the Latino prison gang culture, and especially as it pertains to kids. Not only are young men not afraid to go to prison, but they are expected to, and sometimes demanded to, in order to know if they can be trusted, and whether they are "real soldiers." Imagine being born and raised by that way of life. Would you be strong enough to escape it and find a better way, if that was the only way you had ever known—as a little boy? I know I wouldn't have been. These men have helped me understand humanity in a whole new light, and from a different perspective.

On one trip, while doing my work in a prison, a trusted friend who is serving a life sentence came to see me. He slipped me a note and said, "If you really want to understand the game, just call this number tonight at 7:00 p.m." I asked what it was, and he said, "Just make the call, you'll see." That evening, very curious, I dialed the number. I could immediately tell it was a conference call, but I didn't know who it was or what it was for. I honestly thought it was probably an organization who helped prisoners or someone I needed to connect with. I beeped in and began to listen. *Beep, beep, beep-beep-beep-beep . . . beep, beep, beep-beep.* More callers jumped on the line. Soon there were around thirty people on the call. The host began to call roll and it began to dawn on me who I was listening to. These weren't volunteers or employees, and this was no non-profit organization, however it was organized. The first clue was that all the captains on this call had interesting nicknames. Now, I've been on a lot of conference calls, but never one where everybody had a cool name! This was a large, national gang having their weekly conference call with the gang leaders for all the prisons in that state. I froze. Should I hang up? My heart raced, and I decided that I had to stay on the line and learn the game my friend had wanted me to experience firsthand. When would I ever get another chance like this to see behind the curtain? I was amazed. If you would have joined the call halfway through, you would have thought it was a corporate call. There was no cussing, no interrupting, no threats or challenges; there were rules, and regulations, and standards. They discussed new guidelines that had been passed, and new decisions handed down from on high. They discussed things such as monthly taxes, how to handle violations, when to, and when not to, put their hands on someone, and how to handle brothers who were late on their dues. Once again, it wasn't what I thought it would be. There were very few violations that called for violence, for they had created better ways to handle internal conflict, and even conflicts with other gangs . . . I was mesmerized. All of a sudden there was an unexpected *beep*. The host immediately said, "Identify yourself." No answer. Once again, he said, "Who just got on this call?" Still, no answer. He turned up the volume, and said, "Brother, you'd better identify yourself right now!" For the third time there was no answer, and he said, "Red, Red, Red." Then everyone suddenly jumped off the line—*beep, beep-beep-beep-beep-beep* . . . And one of the first beeps was mine. They had concluded that an officer had seized an illegal cell phone and gotten on the call. I sat there dizzy, and excited at the same time, adrenaline pulsing through my body.

What I learned was that the other side is not playin' around. They have a plan, they are organized, and they are very intentional. All those years

I had spent in the full-time ministry, I had been on few calls that were this organized, and on purpose. I now felt as though we had "played at ministry" while the dark side was churning and burning, and getting things done. That should be a wakeup call for the Church. I had gotten a front row seat to "the Game," but in this game the stakes couldn't be higher. And they were winning.

Tearing Down the Walls That Divide Us

Trapped in a Van in Tijuana

They told me this was a taxi, and they claimed they were taxi drivers. It wasn't, and they weren't. They said, in broken English, that they would take me from the San Ysidro border crossing to the Otay Mesa crossing; they didn't. Alone in the back of a white-panel van, with two Mexican men in the front, the reality of my situation began to set in. Tijuana is currently in the middle of a new cartel war, and it is growing increasingly more dangerous. Tourists do not go there anymore, and kidnappings and murders are on the rise. I looked around the shabby van, and realized I had been fooled. We took a right and went west over a bridge, when Otay is a long drive to the east. When I had gotten into the van, the sliding door was hard to open, and I couldn't get in without assistance. We pulled in to a small parking lot in front of a little store where they wanted me to get more money, stopped the vehicle, and the two men turned around to face me from the front seat. All eyes on me.

"Give us the money," the driver said.

The first words out of my mouth were "I can't," which surprised me.

The man on the passenger side said, "Yes, you can, give us the money."

Again, I replied, "I just can't."

What they said next made absolutely no sense: "Why not?"

Have you ever heard of a hustler, robber, or kidnapper asking the question "why not" after making a demand? They seemed confused. You see, light confuses the darkness. Now, I did not know at this point whether this was a hustle, a robbery, a potential beating, or the worst-case scenario. All I knew was that I could not give them my money. My answer as to why shocked me even more than refusing their request.

I said, and I quote, "Because it's not fair!"

That's right, I appealed to their sense of fairness. I went on to say, "You know I can't give you this money, not even a peso. You said this was a taxi, it isn't. You said you were taxi drivers, you aren't. You said you would take me to Otay, you didn't. If you take me where I need to go, I will give you some money. If I gave you the money now, it just wouldn't be right, and you know that, because you're honorable men." I had learned that honor was very important to males in their culture.

I tried to open the door and it was jammed. I said, "Now let me out of this van."

They sat still and just stared at me. Then I said it a little louder and more sternly: "Let me out of this damn van!" The one in the passenger side got out, opened the sliding door, and I jumped out. I did not run, but I walked with purpose, to a yellow car with the word TAXI on it and I quickly got in (like I should have done in the first place!). The men followed me and stood in front of the car shouting at the driver in Spanish. He went right around them, and we drove away.

On the thirty-minute drive to Otay, in silence, I had time to think about what had just happened, and the way it could have gone. How could I have been so stupid? I'm sure you are wondering the same thing. After crossing that border so many times over the past year, I had gotten way too comfortable in a place where I shouldn't have been comfortable. I asked my friend Ulyses, through an interpreter, why they had let me go. He didn't hesitate and said in Spanish, "Because they thought you were crazy." I guess they were right. The crazy white boy finding himself in another jam, and watching God magically get me out of it once again. But I cannot make the same mistake twice in this game, I must learn. However, I do believe in miracles—how could I not?

Turns out they were probably just two guys with a hustle—but the walls were quickly broken down, and we became just three guys in a van, with a few barriers, trying to relate to one another. If we remove all the drama, baggage, and context, aren't we all just "a few guys in a van" hustling and trying to work things out? Maybe it really is that simple.

Chaidez and the Screwdriver

Jeff's work centers around helping kids get off the streets, stay off the streets, and build a life. We call them "the Boys of Tijuana." Caught in the crossfire of warring cartels, these boys are the toughest, most courageous kids I've ever seen. They laugh easily and play joyfully, but they are tough as nails, and you wouldn't want to cross them. They are brilliant in the ways of the streets, and incredibly gifted on the soccer field. One of the boys is named Chaidez. He's a good player, a tough kid, and used to be an excellent car thief. The Boys of Tijuana took him away from that life, but he laughs when you ask him if he's a good thief. These boys go to great lengths to play on Jeff's team, which is called Letics Sports. They practice twice a day: early in the morning before school, after school, and into the evening. Many of them must also work to try to support their families, and not choose the easy way out and sell drugs for the cartels. Soccer is everything to them, because it's their family, and their protection. Early one morning, while it was still dark, Chaidez was walking to practice, a long way, like he does every day—twice. All of a sudden a robber jumped out of the bushes brandishing a screwdriver. This older man demanded Chaidez's cell phone. The boy calmly reached into his pocket and pulled out six pesos. He looked straight at the man, smiled, and said, "Yes, I would love to buy your screwdriver." He put the pesos in the man's hand, reached over and took the screwdriver, and simply walked away. The bandit stood there confused and speechless, and Chaidez threw the screwdriver into the bushes and walked on to practice. The only way we even found out about it was because Jeff asked him to describe a typical day to us. So, he just shared something that had happened that morning. I share that story with prisoners and they are amazed. Could it really be that simple, to handle conflict calmly and use your head rather than your fists? The most powerful things in life are simple.

Jeff has discovered a secret. Sports are the world's common denominator and peacemaker. Iran can play Israel in the World Cup, and for three magical hours, they don't want to kill each other. And that works all over the world. Why? Because it's up close and personal. I told you, it's hard to hate up close; hate happens at a distance. If you get close enough to competitively crash into one another in a noble contest, it's hard to go back to hating each other quite so quickly after the match is over. We could transform entire prison systems through sports—that is, if transforming a broken system was the goal of those in power.

So that's how they get into a world that is very hard to get into. A middle-aged, white guy from San Diego, accepted on the streets of Tijuana, through sports. When they get close enough to see God in Jeff, they love him. Jeff found a best friend down there named Ulises Romero. He is a former Mexican professional soccer player, and he is the reason the Boys of Tijuana are a family. I played soccer all the way into college, and I've never seen a better soccer coach in my life. He loves these kids so much. At times there are ten or twelve of these boys living with Ulises and Xochilt and their two little girls, in their tiny, little home. That's what family does. Because of Jeff's friendship with Ulises, he is protected from the cartels and by the cartels. Ulises has respect from the right people, but has lived a clean life—a very difficult thing to do. He and Jeff have gotten me out of some tough spots down there because of who they are. If I was running around down there by myself, I think they would probably "deal with me." But the interesting thing is, because I've gone down there to see them so many times, if I was there all alone, I would have family— and family protects one another. So, I would be safe. Relationships and family are the strength and the protection from evil and harm. And just maybe we can come to understand why we are losing so many kids to the streets, on both sides of the border. Perhaps it is because, oftentimes, the streets are showing them more love, and being more of a family, than the churches do. Thank God for Ulises Romero.

Chava's Field

Jeff had an idea that we should feed a poor neighborhood in an area called Terrazas. This area is rough and poor. There are few paved roads, and the area can be very dangerous, and hard to get a taxi to take you to this particular area. Some of the Letics soccer players live there, both boys and girls. There were numerous girls from Terrazas kidnapped, and some killed, over the months that I was down there. Some of the Boys of Tijuana stood guard on the street corners, and walked the female players home from school and practice to protect them. It got so bad that rival cartels were accusing the other of snatching the girls, because nobody knew who was doing it. It turned out to be, most likely, an Asian human-trafficking ring from what we were told. Just think about how dark and sinister that level of evil is, when they can kidnap girls for sex trafficking right under the noses of not one, but two powerful cartels. That sounds like the Devil himself. So, this is the spot Jeff picked. Why? Because the field these boys and girls play soccer on lay right in the middle of this neighborhood.

It was a great idea, but you can't just throw a party on someone's field, in an area like that, without permission. I got in trouble once because I was running around on that same field taking pictures of graffiti walls, and making the bad guys very nervous. Ulises had to come and get me out of there, rather quickly—and that was just me acting a fool. Imagine what they would do if we threw a party on their field without their blessing. So, Ulises got in touch with the right people and set up a meeting with the drug dealer who was in charge of that area. The problem was that this man had recently fled and left town to get away from the cartels (the same way the one before him had). So, we had to meet with the new guy who had just been put in charge, but he was younger than his predecessor. His name is Chava, and he was twenty-five at the time. The meeting was set, and we made our way to the dirt field in Terrazas. It was like a movie. We walked out onto that dusty field on one end, and he walked onto the field from the other end, and we met in the middle. We had a friend named Jesus interpreting for us. (That's right, "Jesus" was our translator.) Jesus has become a great friend, as we have literally preached together many times in prisons and on the streets. He translates and delivers my message with passion—it's like a dance.

As we came together on the field, Jesus began by telling Chava why we were there and why we wanted to meet with him. We treated him with respect, looked him in the eye, shook his hand firmly, and got close enough to connect. We managed to find common ground with a very dangerous young man, on his turf, because we walked with him, and talked with him, and humbled ourselves, and asked for his blessing and permission. Two American men, in their early fifties, requesting a favor from a cartel soldier less than half their age. Interestingly, it was my tattoo that sealed the deal. He pointed at it, and nodded as if to say, "What does that mean?" That's all he had to say. I went on to tell him it was my life story, and the entire sleeve is all about peace. I even showed him the spot that says Paz, which is his word for peace. I made a joke about getting his girlfriend Lupita's name tattooed on my arm, and he laughed. The connection had been made, and we even gave each other the "Gangster Hug" as we departed (you never give a man like that a chest-to-chest hug!). I will never forget Chava's Field. The following day we filled that soccer field with children, music, soccer, tacos, and wonderful fellowship. Chava didn't want to come out to see us, so we went to him. We took him a plate of tacos and gave him full credit for feeding the neighborhood, which made him feel noble. It was beautiful, and I even got to meet Lupita. Then I told Chava that when I came back I was going to have his face tattooed on my chest! He laughed even harder at that one. We had made a friend. The next month we went back to see him, and found that he had been arrested for murder and given forty years at the notorious

La Mesa prison, a prison we had become very familiar with. We had lost Chava, but walls had been broken down, and we were inside where we could do God's work. We have many walls on this side of the border as well, ones that are high and very thick. It's time to tear them down, one brick at a time.

Building the Bridges That Unite Us
The Magnificent Men of La Mesa

The whole reason that Jeff reached out to me in the first place was to see if I would do my work inside La Mesa prison in Tijuana. He knew that many of the kids the Letics team were reaching out to had family in there, and I was the only one he had heard of who was doing that kind of work. La Mesa became infamous in 2008 when five thousand prisoners took over the prison, set it on fire, and held it off and on for almost a month. Eventually troops and tanks were brought in to put down the siege. Many lives were lost, many more than what was reported in the media, according to a man who was there, who happened to be the one who actually set the fire. We met one night, and I interviewed him in the dark by the soccer field. He's a good man, and is raising a good son, and he shared with me what really went on back then. He said they had told him to set the fire, but then it got out of hand. This was the prison Jeff wanted to launch our Power of Peace Project in, and I was stoked.

I cannot tell you why, but I get a high, a real rush, when I get to go into a prison I've never been in before, especially on the foreign mission field. The rougher, the better. It's probably because that is where I have always seen His power the mightiest, and where I have witnessed the most miracles, the unexpected and unexplainable. La Mesa would become another field of dreams, and a miracle factory. We just had to get close enough to see it. You can't see true miracles from a distance; once again, you've got to get up close and personal. That means we must begin building bridges, rather than more walls and tunnels.

Julio and the Mint

We launched the Power of Peace at La Mesa with fifty men from the block they were having the most trouble with, out of five thousand prisoners. The reason we only had fifty is because they will not let more than fifty gather together for programs. At La Mesa these men are stuck in cells fifteen to twenty at a time, and they rarely if ever get out. They must deal with one another in a cell that has bed space for only half of the men in it. They must figure out who gets a bed, how to eat together, who cleans the cell, when to bathe, and when use the bathroom, but in the space of a small room. Keep in mind these fifteen men might be from different gangs or cartels, all jammed in a small space, having to handle conflict and everything else together. That is where Chava is now.

We spent two of the most amazing days together as we laughed, cheered, cried, and even hugged with these men who are demonized. We all became friends and it changed their world, as well as ours. They spent forty days going through our program together, and meeting once a week as a group. We had our *Forty Days to Freedom* book translated into Spanish, and they all took the nonviolent pledge together. One day there was an issue. A brother raised his hand and stood up and said, "We need to pray for Julio. He's all alone." We asked how he could be all alone when everyone was packed in cells together. He said, "No, I mean he is all alone—there are no Power of Peace brothers in his cell. We need to pray for him." I was in awe. In less than a month, they had come to feel as though Julio was all alone, because he wasn't with any of his POPP brothers. It was a magical moment. There was another . . . One of the brothers went to a church service one day (though many of the brothers would skip church to come to the Power of Peace meetings) and the preacher gave every man a mint, like the ones we have that are red and white, with a clear plastic wrapper. That's a big treat in this place. What did he do? He took that mint back to his cell and broke it into fifteen tiny little pieces so that every man could taste the sweetness. Wow. Does that shatter the picture of the cartel members you have heard about and read about in the media? There is no doubt there is evil out there, and that the cartels are some of the most violent and dangerous people on the planet. I'm just telling you what I witnessed up close. Real men, raised in a very tough area, being forced to live like animals, rising above and caring for one another and sharing, rather than stealing. I've never seen anything like it in all the other prisons I've been in.

For our 41st Day Celebration, we had a party. We had pizza, Snickers bars, and Cokes, and families could attend. We had mothers sharing how they had gotten their sons back. One shared how her son had never told her he loved her, and now he was saying it almost every day. Once again, my perspective had changed. All I saw were mothers with their sons, like they were little boys again. During the celebration, the most beautiful song rang out. One of the older brothers had gone over to a mother and began to serenade her with a voice that sounded like an opera soloist. At first, we laughed, but then we listened and admired what this gentleman suitor was respectfully doing for this woman. He went on and on, and she giggled and blushed. It was beautiful. I could tell many more stories about the things God has allowed me to see. I have no idea why He chose me for this ministry, but I'm sure glad that he did. Bridges were being built, and feared and forgotten men were finding true freedom, for freedom is an inside job. And isn't that what we all want for those who have torn down so many beautiful things around us? Maybe not . . .

I was recently told by a particular state's Department of Corrections Commissioner that my services were no longer needed. All the wardens in that state were told not to allow me "behind the wire" any longer. It wasn't a rumor. I was told by someone who was at the meeting with the commissioner when he brought it up, and then confirmed by a warden who received the directive. (You're not paranoid when they really are talking about you!) The reason? We cannot unite and empower dangerous men who might use that power for harm. Aren't they already doing that?

Whether it be the civil rights movement in America, apartheid in South Africa, or Gandhi's colonized India, the powers that be will never be motivated to change a broken system, if it is still working financially for those who created it. It must be dismantled from the inside out by those who are oppressed. It is the same with this young generation that shows so much promise, but faces such perilous threats. They must *be* the change they wish to see; they just need some inspiration. It is time for the people of the light to start uncovering our own tunnels, tearing down our own walls, and building new bridges, so that we can shine the light on the path our brilliant youth wish to travel down.

A New Pathway

If we ever needed to try a different path, it is now. In my fifty-plus years on the planet, I personally have not seen the nation divided to the extent that it is now. I know there have been darker times in our country's fascinating history, but I haven't witnessed it myself, until now. Everyone wants you to choose a side, pick a party, join the fight, and put on a label: red or blue, black or white, conservative or liberal, legal or illegal, rich or poor, gay or straight, Christian or Muslim, Crip or Blood, Alt-right or Antifa . . . and the list keeps growing. I refuse to pick a side, because I refuse to be labeled; as it has been said, "When you label me, you negate me." With such a growing polarity, and an ever-increasing divide, we must remember that the kids are watching, listening, and learning. If uninterrupted, this young generation will grow up basically taking the same position as their parents, as most of us did, and the rift will only get wider. Politically, religiously, socially, and racially, we will have raised a generation driven to dig in and fight for their position harder than ever before—with an increasing level of hatred and violence. What is the solution? Who is teaching them compassion? Where is the empathy? When and where is the next young peace movement going to emerge? Where is the next King, Gandhi, or Mandela? Who is the next Mother Teresa or Maya Angelou? There IS a solution, but not necessarily where we have been looking for it. What if the kids showed us the way? This young generation, Gen Z, is poised to change the world. However, they need some new role models, ones they can relate to, who speak their language, and are willing to LISTEN and help them discover their brilliance. It's time to build some new bridges, over all the hate and judgment, and connect rather than divide. It's time to cut a new path, and have this young generation rise up and take their rightful place of leadership. It is the natural order of things.

Protecting the Dream

Having witnessed what Jeff and Ulises were doing in Tijuana, and the effect it is having on the kids and families there, I got to work on a new book and program in Atlanta. I called it "Protect the Dream." This young generation has never had a movement of their own, and they know very little about the history of movements that have changed the world with previous generations. They need to be inspired to dream, and dream big. All these years later, they still know what Martin said way back in 1963 on the steps of the Lincoln Memorial: "I have a dream." That's how powerful those four words are, and that's why they know it, even if they don't understand it yet. The word dream carries powerful energy, and it can carry you through hardships, loss, suffering, and temptation. The problem is that very few young people these days have big dreams for their lives, so anything "bright and shiny" that gets their attention, moves them. And they have more bright and shiny temptations coming at them than ever before. If we can help them dream big, and wrap value around that dream, then we can teach them to protect that dream at all costs. Having become "Dream Protectors" for themselves, they can then begin to protect the dreams of their fellow students.

Overdose, self-harm, accidental death, and suicide are reaching epidemic levels as kids are trying to deal with their pain in all the wrong ways. Violence, crime, bullying, and date rape have become shockingly common in this Gen Z culture. Through music, video games, and movies that glorify sex and violence, their minds and hearts are becoming numb to these "Dream Killers." The weak and vulnerable students are at great risk, as they are being driven harder and harder to fit in and be what they think is cool. Social media serves to create even more insecurity, as students try to measure up and keep up with the popular kids. We need to change what cool looks like in the classrooms and hallways across this country. However, in the same way the prisoners had to change things for themselves, these students must create the world in which they wish to live. Also, in the same way the inmates who had the most influence had to become positive role models and call different shots, so too must these "in" kids begin to make the change for themselves.

So, I reasoned that the "gang leaders" in our schools are the popular kids, especially the athletes and cheerleaders. If we can get their attention, hold it, and bring about a mind change, then we can get all their followers. These are the kids who are modeling what their peers think is cool: what they wear, watch, listen to, and play; how they walk, talk, and act; what they eat, drink, and smoke; how they treat the opposite sex; and their attitude toward authority. Sports can once again be the beginning of that change, as the athletes are natural leaders and have built-in spectators. So, I created a new forty-day program called "Protect the Dream: 40 Days of Power." It is designed for athletes and competitors, and it focuses on character and leadership development. Every week we tackle a specific Dream Killer with some of the most popular kids in the school, and teach them compassion and acceptance for the other students who are following their lead. These are the seven dangerous Dream Killers:

- Promoting a Bullying Spirit
- Irresponsible Social Media
- Objectifying Classmates
- Unhealthy Relationships
- Disrespecting Authorities

- Alcohol and Drug Abuse
- Lowering Scholastic Standards

Unfortunately, athletes are oftentimes the ones driving these dangerous behaviors. Why? Because that is what they have learned gets them noticed and respected—the things that are trending in their world. And who have they learned it from? The grown folks. They see it from politicians, celebrities, executives, and even parents, teachers, coaches, and preachers. It seems respect, compassion, and integrity have become perceived weaknesses in our culture. What if the young people began to show us the way? Wouldn't that be a kick.

Protect the Dream brings together black kids and white kids, rich kids and poor kids, straight kids and gay kids. They learn to understand the other, find common ground with the other, walk a mile with the other, actively listen to the other, compassionately communicate with the other, apologize and make amends to the other, and to respect the other—even when they disagree. Sounds eerily similar to where this whole thing began. Twelve inmates: black, white, and brown; Christian, Muslim, and Jew; Crip, Blood, Arian Brotherhood, and Latin King. An impossible dream with a group of young rivals, who showed us that if it can happen there, it can happen anywhere. They took away our excuses, and now it has come full circle.

The Promise

All along the way, with thousands of inmates, on four continents, and over half of these United States, I continued to make a promise: If they would become positive role models, then I would carry their message and example to kids on the streets, and to communities in the free world—and that gave them a noble purpose, which many of them lacked. I would live their dream for them, until they could get out and live it for themselves. And it has finally come to fruition. We had a graduation recently where one of the original twelve, who has been released, shared his testimony to a group of students who were completing our Protect the Dream campaign at their 41st Day Celebration. Nicholas is now living HIS dream. I am amazed at all God has done over this past decade—we truly have come all the way back to where we began. These hated, feared, and forgotten men have indeed become positive role models, and now some of them are getting out and carrying their dream "Beyond the Wire."

I believe this is the medicine for a divided nation. If we will simply walk a mile, ask a specific question, listen intently, ask another question, and then keep walking together, then tunnels can be uncovered, walls can be broken down, and bridges can be built. Don't judge, just walk; slow down, don't run, and simply observe with fascination. And please don't say it can't happen in today's drama-filled world. I've seen it on death row; I've seen it in the midst of a gang war; I've even seen it with rival cartels. So, don't tell me it can't work in Congress. Don't tell me it can't work with Christians and Muslims. Don't tell me it can't work between blacks and whites, because I won't believe you. I've seen too much, and I still believe in miracles. Do you?

CHAPTER 24
THE WALK UP AUBURN AVENUE

My son was a college student at Georgia State University. The college is located in downtown Atlanta and is literally walking distance from the neighborhood where Dr. King was born, the church he and his father preached in, and the place where he is buried. The university is on the west side of Interstate 75 which runs right through the middle of the city, and the historic King District on Auburn Avenue is on the east side of I-75. I stopped by and picked up Cole and his best friend Ralph, explaining that I was taking them on a "walking field trip." As we walked under the Auburn Avenue Bridge, where many homeless people live, we passed into the other side of the neighborhood. I wanted to give them a King tour, but more importantly to introduce them to a whole world that they thankfully do not know: the world of the streets.

I have gotten very accustomed and comfortable working with the least of these, and I wanted my son to learn how to handle encounters with beautiful people who do not look like him. So, we began our fascinating walkabout. As we walked up Auburn Avenue toward the historic King home, we encountered two fascinating gentlemen sitting on a stoop. I made eye contact and said, "How do you do, sir?" and gave a confident head nod. He answered back and I extended my hand and introduced myself. One said he was called Lucky and the other was Ricky. As we moved past, Ricky rose and walked toward me asking if I could help him out. I told him that I honestly did not have any cash on me, which he shook off and asked a second time. I again told him I couldn't help him, and he shook his head and muttered an expletive. I turned toward Ricky and asked a question: "How do you know if you can trust someone, Ricky?" He shook his head and said he didn't know. "Just trust him," I replied. "If you are here on this corner in thirty minutes, then you will find out if I am a man of my word. I'll hook you up on my way back." He shook his head and walked away.

We continued up to Dr. King's house, and then back by the King Center where we paid respects to Dr. King and Coretta King, before walking down to historic Ebenezer Church, where Martin and his father had preached many years before. All of this was fascinating for my son and his friend Ralph who had no idea that they lived so close to all of this rich civil rights history. We stopped to film and quickly heard a loud rebuke coming from up the street. A large officer was heading our way quickly, and he seemed to be very upset that we were filming on the grounds. "You cannot film here, you're breaking the law!" he shouted. Unaware of the laws in the King District, I quickly put the camera away and apologized profusely as he got near us. I stretched out my hand and introduced myself and the boys and told him why we were there. I informed him that I was trying to teach this young generation about Dr. King's dream and that we meant no disrespect. He proudly informed us that he was a marine and how he had worked in the district for years. I stopped and looked at my son and said, "You boys need to listen to this man, he fought for our country so that we can be free." The officer straightened up tall and looked even more dignified. He said, "Young men, you need to listen to your father." We walked away, and as we went, he yelled, "Thank you for what you are doing, sir," surprising my young companions.

As we ventured on down past the corner, I didn't see Ricky. I looked across the street and saw Lucky hanging out in front of a liquor store with a bunch of young guys with absolutely nothing but time on their hands in the middle of the day. I hollered at him, "Yo, Lucky, where's Ricky?" He whistled up the street and pointed toward me. Ricky saw me and came running down the road. As he reached us, I dug into my pocket pulling out a five dollar bill, handed it to him, and said, "I told you that you could trust me, sir." He smiled and shook his head in disbelief. At that moment a voice came shouting from across the street on the corner, "You see that, fellas? There goes an honorable man!" I was being vouched for by on-looking strangers that most people might instinctively fear. I imagine that the next time I pass that way, those young men will remember me, and who knows, they might even protect me if need be.

As we walked back under the bridge to the other side of the world, we talked about the lessons we had learned on that field trip: always look a man in the eye and call him "sir." Don't walk the other way in fear, but rather nod your head with respect. Show respect to law enforcement and authorities, because they have a very tough job and you never know the price that they have paid. And always be a man of your word and do what you tell people that you are going to do—they will respect you for that, especially on the streets. Then I looked at them both very sternly and said, "Promise me that you will never do this without me, but now you know how to handle yourself if trouble finds you." All of these were just more valuable lessons that I learned from my brothers on the inside.

Releasing of the Doves

I was recently invited to speak at a very special gathering. The event was held outdoors at a beautiful park in Atlanta. There were vendors, a catered lunch, and beautiful decorations along the trees, tents, and gazebos. There was live music and crafts and children playing at different booths and exhibits. It was very festive, but there was also a very somber feel to this gathering group of beautiful people. I was asked to speak alongside a pastor, a spiritual teacher, and a rabbi. I was honored to have been invited and eager to offer my help. This was no ordinary gathering, as all of the participants had one thing in common: they had all lost a child to suicide. I was humbled and apprehensive, wondering if I would have the right words to say to these incredible survivors and overcomers.

I spoke from the heart and told them of my amazing journey. I spoke of the loss of my father, which was ruled as an accidental overdose, though we would never really know for sure what had happened that night. I spoke of my own struggle with the disease of addiction and how it had led me through my pain and into my passion and life purpose. I spoke of the loss and wreckage of the broken lives that I get to witness God putting back together. I spoke of the families who had healed from devastating tragedy, and how we never really get over it, but how we can learn to live with it day by day. I didn't try to speak to something of which I do not know, but I shared my heart and tried to be present and available. They responded with love, laughter, and genuine gratitude. Once again I was blown away. However, it was what happened at the end of the day which made the biggest impression.

They had set up a place down by the lake where people could buy doves—beautiful, soft, white doves: the symbol of peace. They were all in little crates and you could purchase them, with all the proceeds going to a wonderful charity that ministers to families who have tragically lost their little loved ones. We were all preparing for one of the most beautiful and powerful ceremonies that I have ever been a part of; I just didn't know it yet.

I received my dove and held it in my hands. It felt so soft and vulnerable, like I was going to hurt it if I wasn't careful. I waited as everyone came together into a big, beautiful group with doves in hand. A woman stepped forward and offered the most beautiful prayer and then a special song was played. I knelt and said a prayer to the little dove that was in my hands. I asked it to carry a special message to my father, and to all the loved ones who have gone on ahead of us. The doves represented the souls of the children who were being mourned by all the grieving families present that day. When we released the doves, we were releasing their spirits into the universe to bring light and healing to the nations. I didn't know what to expect, for I had never done this before. As I rose from my prayer, I released the dove and it flew off along with all the rest. The sound of all the wings fluttering together made the most amazing and beautiful sound. The doves quickly came together in a tight formation and began to fly around and around in a sweeping pattern. They would fly high and then swiftly come swooping down as one, as if to do a "fly by" just for us.

The feeling of power that left my body as I released the dove is something that I will never be able to fully explain or describe. The rush was so intense that it literally took my breath away, almost lifted me off of my feet, and a giggle burst out of me. Then I broke into tears of joy mixed with pain and hope all at the same time. All I know is that it was a powerful and magnificent moment, and one that I will treasure always. We all mingled and embraced in silence, and then we all went our separate ways, forever changed. This is why I do what I do. All of this ties together: alcohol, drugs, addiction, overdose, incarceration, and suicide. We are all just trying to deal with pain in various ways and trying to find comfort—many times in the wrong places. There is a better way, and there is so much work yet to be done. Let us continue to bring healing to those who desire it.

This has been an amazing ride and we've just gotten started. It all changed that one night years ago when I walked into a jailhouse to visit with my young friend Luis. Well, now we come full circle and we finish this book where it all began. After all these years, I was in a Federal Courthouse in downtown Atlanta testifying on behalf of Luis, right before the Judge handed down his long-awaited sentence. I shared before the court how his courage and transformation planted the seeds which would become the Power of Peace Project. I told the judge that if I hadn't first seen it in him, someone who I already knew, then I wouldn't have believed that it was even possible. If I hadn't witnessed his refusal to fight with the officers or his rivals anymore, and seen him put his life on the line for his faith, then I wouldn't have caught the vision for what POPP could become. For eight long years he has waited for this day. He has been transferred from one facility to another, in maximum security, many times in isolation, and now here we were. I sat with his mom and anxiously awaited the decision which would be handed down to determine his fate. His attorney told us that he has never seen such security in a courtroom. We were asked to stand and the judge began to deliver his decision. The deal that he had accepted was for thirty years to life in a federal penitentiary. Luis is now thirty years old. The judge explained that he was taking into account the fact that Luis had cooperated with the government in his case and that he understood how that decision has put his life in grave danger. He told us that our testimony about his transformation and what he did to help create POPP also had an important impact on his decision. And now the sentence was read: Luis was given twenty years and credit for the eight years he had already served. If he serves good time then he will be released before he is forty years old. I assured the court that I will have a place for him in my organization upon his release. This part of the journey is complete and the next season in Luis's courageous life begins. I will be there for him during this final stretch until we meet again one day in the free world.

This journey has taken me around the world and I've met some of the most fascinating people on the planet: Birdie Boy, Andre, Sir Brown, Dae Dae, Miami, Leonid, Johnny, Potts, Lynch-Bey, and so many more. This idea became an experiment, which led to a program that then evolved into a movement. Today, thousands of convicts and students across the country are taking a stand for peace in their communities. They carry the torch for the Champions of Peace who went before them. They are the true heroes of this book, and the ones who might have gone unnoticed — until now. They're the jock who stands up for the weak student on the playground, the prisoner who encourages a new inmate who is afraid, the brother who gives some of his food to a convict who is hungry, the popular girl who eats lunch with the misfit, the cool kid who makes friends with the nerd, the gang leader turned peacemaker, and the bully transforming into the defender. This young generation is ripe for a peace movement, and now they've got one of their very own; surprisingly, it was inspired by hated, feared, and forgotten men who have proven that God is not done with them yet.

Everyone wants peace, and it never goes out of style—the peacemaker is now cool in school. And hope really is the new dope: you can't do too much, getting hooked is a good thing, and this high never ends. Take a stand and join the Power of Peace Movement. Take hold of peace and don't let it go. Grab it, hang on to it, and lift it high. Then share it with someone who really needs it—we all do. And peace be with you brothers and sisters, along this wonderful journey. I'll see you on the field.

POPP
JOIN THE MOVEMENT

I'm so grateful that you have invested your valuable time in reading *Peace Behind the Wire: A Nonviolent Resolution.* Now the question is what can YOU do to make a difference in your community? First, make a firm decision to get involved in helping at-risk youth one way or another in your neighborhood (and in today's world there are no kids who aren't at risk). Second, choose the area in which you would like to help. Once you begin to investigate the volunteer opportunities for youth in your community, you will be amazed at all the current needs. Third, do something TODAY that signifies your commitment to change. Yesterday is history, and tomorrow is a mystery—all we have is today. Don't put it off and decide that "someone else will handle it." Maybe they won't, and another day goes by.

I want to encourage you to go to PowerofPeaceProject.com and get involved. Watch a video, subscribe to our monthly newsletter, follow our weekly blog, or listen to our weekly "Power of Peace Radio Show." Buy a t-shirt, make a donation, or volunteer for one of our programs in your area. Reach out to a kid who you know is on a dangerous path and direct them to us—we specialize in interrupting and redirecting teens who are wandering, drifting, or running down a dangerous path. When you visit our site, be sure to send us a message and let us know you were there, and let us know that you wish to help. In this field there is no competition, only collaboration, because the problem is far too big for any of us to tackle on our own.

Join the Power of Peace Movement today. Through our youth, we can change the world—one soul at a time. They are our future, so we must engage them TODAY. And to all the young people out there: You have proven that you are not afraid to die. Now, choose to truly live. Dream BIG, and protect that dream at all costs.

Peace,

Kit Cummings
Founder & President
Power of Peace Productions, Inc.

ABOUT THE AUTHOR

Kit's presentations are dynamic, thought-provoking, fun, and energy-filled. Built around timeless universal laws and principles, Kit's programs help individuals find inner peace, teams to come together, leaders to emerge, innovative solutions to be realized, and inner potential among participants to be fulfilled—with laughter and inspiration as the catalyst.

As an inspirational author, cutting-edge teacher, and international speaker, Kit Cummings delivers a timely message of unlimited human power and potential. With a personal and professional pursuit of coaching and developing people for over twenty-five years, Kit has created a unique approach to address the most pressing and fundamental issues surrounding personal and collective achievement in a program he calls Attitude Science. Combining this with his captivating gift for entertaining and engaging his audience, Kit dynamically imparts the most thought-provoking and profound truths of the human experience, with incredible takeaways. Kit's message is timely and relevant, transcending the mundane day-to-day grind and offering cutting-edge perspectives and tools that motivate and empower teams and organizations to greater heights. Attitude Science helps participants break through barriers and achieve powerful results.

Born and raised in Atlanta, Kit has been involved in the field of personal development and leadership for over two decades. He earned a BBA in marketing from the Terry School of Business at the University of Georgia, and he also holds a Master of Theology. Kit is the president and founder of Power of Peace Project, Inc. and brings his experience working in some of the most dangerous areas in the world to bring about organizational change. Kit has inspired people to aim higher in places as far away as Africa, Asia, Latin America, and Europe, and recently completed speaking tours in South Africa, Mexico, Honduras, and Ukraine. Kit has negotiated peace between rival gang leaders in dangerous prisons and has spoken at the Gandhi Global Peace Summit in Durban, South Africa. Having taught in some of the toughest environments in the world and to some of the roughest audiences, he now brings his dynamic message to corporate conferences, seminars, and workshops. Book Kit today and prepare your people to be inspired, motivated, and entertained.

PowerofPeaceProject.com